DAVID A. STONE

2

Nothing Happens Till Somebody Sells Something

DAVID A. STONE

BRISA BOOKS

Brisa Books/
WindWord Communications Inc.
#509, 4438 West 10th Avenue
Vancouver, British Columbia, Canada
www.brisabooks.com

ISBN-10:0987727478
ISBN-13:978-0-9877274-7-3

This book is dedicated to all the Marketing Coordinators in the AEC industry who start early, stay late and do their best to turn technical jargon into persuasive client engagement

FOREWORD

Following the Great Recession, as design professionals slowly crawled out from under the rocks where they'd been hiding, they re-emerged into an unfamiliar place. Whereas before you could count on the sustained loyalty of a good client, suddenly everything was going through the purchasing department. Whereas before, the founding Partners had all the great relationships, suddenly they were choosing to retire and leave business development in the unsure hands of the next generation of leaders.

A lot changed during that disruptive period and we now operate in a different world. A world in which top-notch technical capability is assumed and consultant selection criteria are often intangible. A world in which giant firms compete for miniature projects and the local firm is left wondering what happened.

A world in which smart, sophisticated marketing is a critical success factor.

This book will help you navigate that different world. It will explain why things are the way they are and what your firm can and should do in response. It will give you the big picture and the nitty-gritty details of an action plan. It will tell you informative stories and draw out the lessons-learned. In short, it will give you what you need to know to find your way through this unfamiliar territory.

This new world might be unfamiliar, but it doesn't have to be scary. Armed with the marketing and business development strategies and tactics in this book, your firm can adapt, grow and thrive. No, things ain't like they used to be. In many ways, they're a whole lot better!

CONTENTS

ACKNOWLEDGMENTS

This book and, in fact, all the work I do in consulting, coaching, training and writing, would not be possible without the fabulous AEC firms across the country that I am privileged to call my clients. I'm convinced that I learn more from them than I'm ever able to give back.

All this would be equally impossible without the daily support, encouragement and astoundingly keen insight of my beautiful wife and partner, Gail. Thank you!

GO/NO GO ECONOMICS

I'd like to kick off this marketing book by advising you to back off on how much you're marketing. That might seem a little bizarre but just about every firm I know writes and submits way too many proposals.

And wins way too few.

I've joked before about the fact that the easiest way to double your hit rate is to cut in half the number of proposals you submit. But here are some solid financial reasons for cutting back on the number of proposals you write.

Your first step in raising your hit rate is to stop chasing jobs that you're likely to lose. The decision of whether to chase a project or not can be a tough one: If you don't chase it, you're guaranteed not to win it.

But chasing everything that moves is an expensive, time-consuming and frustrating process. This year you're going to get wiser than that and there is a really solid economic argument for cutting way back on the number of proposals you write. Let's look at some hard numbers that ought to convince you to back off on your proposal activity.

Proposal costs vary widely depending on the size of the project, the degree of competition and the expectations of the client. But let's assume that your average cost to produce a competitive proposal is $7,500—a number that's probably close to the middle of the pack in the industry for a competitive proposal.

Let's also assume that your hit rate is 35%—and that might be even a little higher than average in the AE industry.

Based on these two numbers, every project that you win would have to produce a profit of $21,429 for you to just break even on the proposal costs of all the jobs you <u>didn't</u> win.

Now let's assume that you've become quite disciplined and cut way down on the number of proposals you write. Additionally, you spend more time and more money on each one—let's push it to $10,000—

which increases both the quality of your proposals and the likelihood of winning.

Using this strategy, your hit rate jumps up to 80%, which isn't at all unheard of by firms using these best practices. In this case, your breakeven point falls to just $12,500—a little more than half of the previous number.

Let's recap: You cut back on the number of proposals you write, thus easing the pressure on your marketing staff, your marketing costs go down and you use the extra time and resources to raise the quality of your proposals.

The result is that your hit rate and your profits both go up significantly.

PLAYING SHERLOCK HOLMES

Before you zip off another of your standard proposals (the kind where the first step is 'Save As...' from the last proposal) think about this: Do your proposals really zero-in on the needs and circumstances of each client, or do they look and read much the same no matter who they go to?

To laser target your proposal and drive up your hit rate, a little detective work is in order. Your goal is to collect as much information about the client, the project, the selection process, the competition, and the surrounding circumstances as possible.

Here are a couple of classic sleuthing techniques that can turn up a surprising amount of valuable information in a short period of time.

The Six Degrees of Separation
Reporters have always believed that it takes just six steps to connect you with any other human being on the face of the earth. (With LinkedIn and Facebook now it's likely much less than that!)

Let's say I'd like to be introduced to the Director of Facilities of the Acme Corporation. First, I ask someone—anyone—if they know someone who knows the Director and could introduce me. Predictably, they don't. But then I ask if they know anyone who knows anything about the Acme Corporation and might be able to put me a step closer. They remember that their neighbor down the street has a job in a similar industry.

I call the neighbor, explain how I was given his name, and ask if he knows anyone who might be able to help. He's glad to give me the name of a sales rep that regularly calls on Acme. I call the rep and ask him the same question. And on it goes until I get the introduction.

A good journalist can connect themselves to the right information source with a few well-placed phone calls. They whittle down the number of connections by maintaining a thick file of friendly sources they've built up over the years. You haven't been accepting all those LinkedIn invitations for nothing. It's time to start using them to collect and direct you to information.

The Scavenger Hunt
This technique is useful when you have to delegate the information gathering. It can be very effective when you're pressed for time. The object of the game is to see who can collect the most information in a fixed period of time.

Identify two staff members—I've used a Marketing Coordinator and the Receptionist—and explain that their task is to collect as much information about the client, the project, the competition, or anything regarding the project as they can before the time is up. Then give them a tight deadline. A couple of hours works well, but I've used as little as 20 minutes!

Each person has access to a phone and Google. Tell them that they are an ace reporter and they have a hot story due on the Six O'clock news. Then let them go at it. The winner—the one who comes back with the most information—gets dinner for two at the nicest restaurant in town.

I've unearthed some real information gems using these techniques. When you sprinkle those gems throughout your proposal, your presentation and your conversations with the client, you look like a wizard and your win rate skyrockets.

EXCEEDING CLIENT EXPECTATIONS

If I had a nickel for every time I've heard an AE firm tell a prospective client that they will "exceed your expectations" I'd be lying on a beach in Margaritaville.

It's a pretty common phrase and, on the surface, it makes sense. "Not only will we do what you expect, we'll go above and beyond and startle you with the quality of our work and service."

The idea of seeking out regular, reliable and candid feedback from clients is simultaneously exciting and terrifying. It feels great to get the "attaboys" and the glowing testimonials when things go well, but what kind of feedback do you want or get when you screw up? How often do you actively seek your clients' opinions about what you do well and what you do poorly? More importantly, what do you do with those opinions when they're given?

The first lesson in looking for client feedback is a word of caution. Regardless of how you learn what clients think, once they've shared their thoughts they fully expect you're going to do something about it. If you're not prepared to make real changes based on the feedback you receive, don't ask for it. Soliciting opinions and then doing nothing is far worse than failing to ask in the first place. If they had some concerns before, they're downright pissed now.

Informal Feedback
What's the best way to get honest and straightforward opinions? First, you should make it a regular habit to simply ask your clients for their candid views. No formal focus group session, just a quick question at the end of any (or every!) meeting.

- How have we been doing lately?
- Is there anything you'd like to see us improve?

- How are we measuring up against (your competitor's name here) this year?

Continuous, informal feedback allows you to keep your finger on the pulse of your own performance and see how your image is fluctuating.

Formal Feedback

Firms are also finding big value in formally asking clients for their feedback. There are a variety of methods including one-on-one interviews, written or online surveys and focus groups. Each one has its advantages and drawbacks and we don't have the space here to examine each in depth.

But I want to mention a survey process that I think offers more opportunity for regular, honest feedback than I've seen anywhere else. Developed by an architectural firm in Raleigh, NC, the online methods used by *Client Feedback Tool* to get really useful client feedback are worth your time to investigate. Check them out at www.clientfeedbacktool.com.

"We'll exceed your expectations" is a cornball statement that fools no one... unless you can back it up by describing your program to determine, measure and track client expectations and your action plan to respond to them. Set your firm apart by telling your client how your process includes regular client feedback and a project kickoff meeting to identify and quantify their expectations from which your team will establish goals and procedures to go beyond them by a measurable 10%.

Now that's impressive.

RULES ARE MEANT TO BE BROKEN (OR AT LEAST BENT)

M ost RFPs are careful to forbid you from speaking with the members of the selection committee and then go on to lay out a few other rules of the game as well.

There are some real advantages to breaking the rules, the biggest of which is that it might help you win. Let's be clear—I'm in favor of getting all the unfair advantage that's available!

Your first step to bad boy status (and just maybe winning the project) is to read the RFP carefully. Very often there will be language that lays out the rules, but then there'll be a statement to the effect that, 'notwithstanding all these rules, we get to choose who we want anyway.' In my books, when that statement is included, all's fair in love and RFPs.

Let's take that rule about not speaking with the selection committee. At the very least, call or write simply to introduce yourself, let them know that you will be submitting a proposal and are looking forward to dealing with them.

You never know, you just might gain some insight into their thoughts or feelings about the project. If someone does agree to speak with you, don't spend your time selling your firm to him or her. Instead, probe for their thoughts about the project. Listen carefully to what they want to talk about. Begin by asking some probing questions, then spend most of your time listening to the answers. You're likely to make a good impression with your listening skills.

But it's not just committee members who can be useful. Once upon a time I was helping a firm chase a transit hub project. The rules clearly stated that we were not to contact anyone on the selection committee. But one day I was doing some reconnaissance around the area where the project was to be built and came across the city's temporary transit center—a big parking lot with a collection of single-wide trailers where the buses connected and turned around. In the middle of the parking lot, directing traffic and looking very stressed, was the Transit Supervisor. At her next break I offered to buy her coffee. Over the next 15 minutes I gained more insight into the issues surrounding that project than could ever have been gleaned from the RFP or the 'official' sources. All for the price of a much appreciated cup of coffee.

A few days later I got a call from the guy coordinating the RFP, who rapped my knuckles for bending the rules. I apologized profusely (nudge, nudge, wink, wink) and we went on to win the job.

Always check the rules. Then think about the advantages and consequences of bending or breaking them. Yes, it can be risky. But if you can win some truly valuable insight, or make a positive impression during your conversations, that risk may well be worth it.

HOW'S YOUR MARKETING PLAN GOING SO FAR?

OK, that was a cheap shot. But take a look at the calendar and see what month this is. If it's April, and if things are going the way they should, you ought to be 1/3rd of the way towards implementing your plan to win a steady supply of profitable work. If it's August, you should be 2/3rd of the way there.

If you don't have a documented marketing plan, you're not alone. My highly unscientific research tells me that most firms don't. And if they do, it's questionable at best and probably collecting dust on a shelf rather than informing day-to-day actions.

Your marketing plan doesn't have to be big and complicated. In fact, short and simple are much better traits if you want it to be actionable. Of the plans that are developed, too many are large, cumbersome things, filled with way too much research and market studies and far too little action. Think of it as a plan of action—"Monday morning we do this. When we're finished, we move on to that." You should be able to summarize a perfectly reasonable plan on a single page.

Here's what your marketing plan needs to contain:

➤ Here's what we sell—a description of our services. This is what we bring to the market that sets us apart—the things that differentiate us from our competitors and make it worthwhile for our clients to seek us out.

➤ Here are our competitors and how we stack up against the strengths, weaknesses and differentiators of each one.

➤ Here's who we sell to—a description of our target markets including geographic reach, market sectors, industries and agencies, typical client profile, traits of our ideal client.

➤ Here are the actions we take to build and maintain our brand in the market—this part isn't about winning projects, it's about creating name recognition, enhancing reputation and building 'mind share' across our target markets. We do this to get the attention of that client who doesn't know us yet but is going to hire us two years from now.

➢ Here are the actions we take to build and create one-to-one relationships. This describes our client 'schmoozing' activities that build those important trust-based relationships.

➢ Here are the actions we take to win particular projects. This describes our proposal and presentation strategies including go/no go decision making, win strategy development, proposal writing and presentation development.

➢ Here are the actions we take to ensure our current clients keep coming back. These are our customer service strategies that shape the experience our clients have while working with us.

➢ Here are the tools we use to get this all done. This is our marketing infrastructure including staff, space, hardware and software, libraries, resources, etc.

➢ Here is how much this is all going to cost. This is our marketing budget for the year including salaries both direct and indirect, equipment costs, project chases, client entertainment and gifts, and all the money we plan to spend to win work.

➢ Here is how we're going to measure our progress. This is the ongoing tracking and monitoring plan to make sure it's working and make adjustments if it's not.

As you can see, most of this you already know. You don't need to conduct exhaustive market research. Sure, it's a good idea to keep tabs on the market and confirm that your assumptions are correct. But it's usually safe to say that you already know 95% of what you need to know. So just sit down and make the plan.

You will not stick to the plan. No one ever does. As Field Marshall Helmuth Carl Bernard Graf von Moltke (you remember him, don't you?) famously said, "No battle plan survives contact with the enemy." But that doesn't mean you shouldn't plan. In fact it's the process of planning, of considering your situations, your options and your best actions that provides the value. The planning process is far more valuable than the plan itself.

So how is the rollout of that plan going? Is it time to make adjustments? Or is it time to make the plan in the first place?

IS IT TIME FOR PLATINUM ELITE PLUS?

Earlier this week I found myself (again!) sitting on a plane and I got to thinking. The first time you buy a ticket on an airline, you pay full fare. No special deals for you, Jack. You wanna fly? Here's the price.

But you're not 10 feet off the ground when the flight attendant comes on the PA and thanks all the frequent flyers for their allegiance, invites the newbies to join, and then describes all the wonderful benefits of being a frequent flyer with Acme Airlines. Free trips, priority boarding, free baggage check, seating upgrades... There is no end to how great life can be when you've demonstrated your loyalty to us.

It's not just airlines that have figured out that giving loyal customers special treatment can pay big dividends. Hotel chains, grocery stores, clothing retailers... Even quickie sandwich shops have a little card that's punched when you buy your lunch.

I'm a living testament to the fact that these programs work. Whenever possible I fly on Delta and stay at a Marriott. Not because they're necessarily better, but because I've reached Platinum status with both and I like the special treatment.

For some reason, we in the design professions have either not got the memo, or we think we know better. Standard practice in the AE world is to low-ball a fee in order to win a new client. Then, after they've shown that they want to work with us on multiple projects, we try to bump the price back up to where it should have been in the first place!

But that practice is simply not sustainable. If the client came to you in response to your low fee, what makes you think they won't do the same thing when the next guy comes along who's willing to undercut you? Maybe it's time to learn from the airlines and offer a formal program that rewards your frequent and loyal clients.

It costs about five to six percent of the fee to land any given project. So offering a discount or providing coupons or vouchers for an equivalent amount of service at no charge when the next project is awarded sole source is easy. You can work out the math and determine what works for you.

As for those arcane rules about not being allowed to provide services for free, you do it all the time anyway! The scope creep that happens on every project is a massive give-away of free services. Why not formalize and control it?

But your loyalty program doesn't need to be just about free services and discounts. Let's get creative and think about special access to Principals: an exclusive 'Client Club' that gathers similar clients in a think tank situation twice a year so they can benefit from each other's experience; perhaps an annual facility inspection; or ... The opportunities for giving special treatment to your special clients are endless.

No, your engineering firm is not a hotel, an airline or a sandwich shop. But like those businesses, you've long known that repeat customers are the best kind. Why not take a lesson from them?

The fact that our industry has never done something like this before is a lousy reason to avoid a good idea. The best marketing ideas are no longer to be found in other engineering firms—we've exhausted that source. Instead, let's look outside this way-too-conservative industry and see what the hotels and grocery stores can teach us.

LEXICAL DENSITY
(TRUST ME, YOU'RE SUFFERING FROM IT)

*O**bject affordances defined by shape and manipulability provide cues such that humans require abbreviated time for object experimentation in order to determine its functionality.*

What!?

(People sometimes know how to use a tool just by looking at it.)

I really like Discover Magazine. Aimed at educated non-professionals, it's intended to be somewhat easier to read than Scientific American but more detailed and science-oriented than magazines like Popular Science. In other words, it's written for people like me who pride themselves on being somewhat intelligent, but who haven't yet got around to finishing that PhD in theoretical physics.

Carl Zimmer, a regular contributor to Discover says, "Anyone who wants to learn how to write about science [or engineering!] should work hard to learn how to explain science in plain yet elegant English."

This is an important lesson for engineers and technical professionals who communicate about their topics to clients in proposals and presentations. This should not be confused with 'dumbing down' or patronizing your audience. It's simply good advice if you want to be understood.

There is a concept in writing called 'lexical density' and it refers to the difficulty of reading any particular passage. This is measured using a tool called the Gunning Fog Index, which uses a combination of paragraph length, sentence length, number of multi-syllable words, and several other factors to measure the readability of English writing. The index estimates the years of formal education needed to understand the text on a first reading. A fog index of 12 requires the reading level of a U.S. high school senior (around 18 years old).

The fog index is commonly used to confirm that text can be read easily by the intended audience. Texts for a wide audience generally need a fog index less than 12. Texts requiring near-universal understanding generally need an index less than 8. The Bible, Shakespeare, Mark Twain, and TV Guide all have Fog Indexes of about 6. Time, Newsweek, and the Wall Street Journal average about 11.

Most of the proposals I review from engineers and design professionals score in the high teens and low 20's. That means you'd need 20 years of formal education in order to easily read and understand them!

Technical professionals pride themselves on their ability to be factual and concise—it comes from being trained in writing technical papers. But this skill does not typically translate well when writing marketing copy.

Tim Radford, a renowned British science writer once said: "Don't overestimate [their] knowledge and don't underestimate their intelligence." Your audience is more than capable of understanding complex concepts, if you explain them. While your audience is intelligent, they will never complain that you've made something easy to understand.

Perhaps the most powerful reminder to keep things simple is the elegant truth that nobody has to put up with reading what you wrote or listening to your presentation. Your audience is there voluntarily. They can (and will!) stand up and walk out any time they choose.

To paraphrase Tim Radford, you are not writing or presenting to impress the professor who got you through your degree, nor the rather dishy person you just met at a party, or even your mother. You are presenting to someone who has 73 other priorities and will walk out in a heartbeat if you give them an excuse. While you may be compelled to write that proposal or give that presentation, nobody has ever felt obliged to read or listen.

THE CURSE OF COMPETENCE

Your firm does really good work. Your buildings don't fall down. Your treatment plants perform to spec. Your control systems operate flawlessly.

Well done, You!

But there's a problem.

Your competitors do really good work too. Competence is everywhere. It's assumed. And it's no longer valued.

Pull out a recent proposal that you've submitted to any client and read through it. You'll discover that you're selling competence. Here's a real example:

Acme Engineering has extensive experience with conducting and reviewing HUD Environmental Assessments in accordance with the National Environmental Policy Act (NEPA) and 24 CFR Part 58. In addition to conducting the Environmental Assessments for 26 projects in Jefferson County worth approximately $210 million, Acme provided quality control reviews for the remaining 41 regional projects in surrounding counties.

Man, are these folks capable! But so are dozens, if not hundreds of other firms. Mere competence isn't what's needed anymore.

What's needed in today's cash-strapped, deficit-ridden, multi-priority and overwhelmingly complicated world is innovative, creative solutions to a whole new class of really sticky problems. How can we replace a crumbling infrastructure when we're up to our ears in debt? Tackle THAT problem and you'll be in demand everywhere.

While it may sound glib, you're doing the easy stuff. You're solving the easy problems. The same problems that thousands of firms can solve.

Are you making a contribution to this new class of really tough tests or are you waiting for someone else to solve them so you can do the easy stuff? Your firm's future depends on these big challenges being solved.

So what unexpected team are you assembling? What non-traditional but vital talents are you adding? What strange bedfellows are you joint-venturing with in order to tackle these unprecedented challenges?

If we wait around for someone else to define the problem, create the scope of work and figure out how to pay for it, there'll be no shortage of talent who are then ready to find a 'solution.' But today's challenges and your firm's future lie in those difficult first three steps. What is your firm doing to play on THAT stage? Someone has to solve these problems. Why not you?

When was the last time you sat down with an economist or an investment banker to see how you might pool talents and resources? When was the last time you included a politician on your team so you could redefine the problem and develop a totally unexpected solution? When was the last time you invited someone whose knowledge area was radically different than yours to bring a new perspective to your firm? When was the last time you stuck your toe into some truly different water?

I can't help but feel that most of us are still waiting for 'normal' to return. It ain't gonna.

You didn't ask the economy to change, but it did. And now it's time to stop blaming it. It's time to stop waiting for prosperity in exchange for competence. It's time to change, to stretch, to go far beyond mere competence and start tackling the really hard problems of today.

You and your team are way beyond competent—you're creative, resourceful and innovative. Can you also be daring?

THANK YOU!

It's really important to say 'thank you' on a regular basis. It's especially important to say thank you to those who allow you to do what you do—in other words, your clients and customers. There aren't many of us (certainly none that I know) who can afford to do this as a hobby. Without a steady supply of regular and loyal clients we'd all be dead in the water.

So THANK YOU to all my readers, all my clients, all the state and national organizations who find it worthwhile to read my blog, buy my books, invite me to deliver seminars and engage me to help them win a steady supply of profitable work for their firms. I can't tell you how much it means to me!

And when was the last time you said 'Thanks!' to your clients? Doesn't have to be a big fancy deal, just a quick word following a meeting, a note or a card or a dinner or a round of golf. Drop off a box of donuts with a thank you note. Do they have a favorite band—why not tickets to a concert? Are they a fan of the local team—how about some great seats at an upcoming game?

Of course there are plenty of clients who can't accept such gifts. For them, simply stop by their office, stick your head in the door and say, 'Just want you to know how much I appreciate your business!' If you say it sincerely with a smile and mean every word, it'll be just as valuable as a pair of tickets at center court.

There isn't a person on this planet who doesn't appreciate being appreciated. So make a note to yourself to thank a client this week. They'll thank you for it!

IS IT TIME FOR ENGINEERING TO BE SEXY?

My first job in this business was as a draftsman at an electrical engineering firm in Toronto in 1974. Drafting boards, mylar sheets, parallel bars and pencils. How far we've come!

It's also interesting to look back from a marketing perspective because at that time it was considered unethical for a firm to publish even a business card as an advertisement. You could get your knuckles rapped for that kind of unprofessional and unfair competitive behavior. How far we've come! Today we've got Cut-your-heart-out-with-a-rusty-knife-and-eat-it-for-breakfast competition.

For about the last twenty years, design professionals have been engaged in a frantic game of catch-up as they've had to learn about marketing in a competitive marketplace. We've attended seminars and symposia and challenged ourselves to think outside our rather rigid boxes. Most of this learning, however, has been from each other. Firms learning from other firms, trading ideas and copying 'best practices' wherever we could find them.

Along the way we've all learned a lot about marketing. We've learned how to build those critical relationships, write engaging proposals, maintain rich websites and deliver compelling presentations.

The unintended result though is that the marketing efforts of the majority of firms today look and feel the same. We've learned so much from each other that we now resemble that little town in the mountains where they just keep marrying each other.

I contend that, from a marketing standpoint, we've learned all there is to learn from each other. The next lessons have to come from outside our industry.

Some years ago I spoke at an AIA conference. My topic was branding as an emerging marketing strategy. Despite the fact that my talk was at the 101 level at best, there were 100 people anxiously taking notes and asking questions. After the session a woman approached me and asked, "Is it just me, or are these people way behind the times?" Turned out that she had just taken over as Marketing Director at an AE firm after 10 years in consumer marketing. She said that the things I'd been discussing, the things that seemed like new news to the crowd, were things the consumer market had been doing for more than 100 years!

There's an important lesson in this—the next big thing for AE marketing isn't going to be found in a case study from another engineering firm, it's hiding in the way they're marketing vacations. Or cars. Or soap. Or insurance.

Things don't get much duller than insurance. And for years the insurance industry sold their services using predictable notions like trust, and solidity, and dependability. Important stuff, but boring as gray paint.

Then some bright bunny (who I hope is really rich today) got the brilliant idea of making insurance sexy. Turns out that he is because that bright bunny was Warren Buffet. He bought Geico in 1996 and turned on the marketing. According to one report, Geico has outspent its competitors in marketing in 16 of the past 17 years. Not coincidentally, it has also increased both profits and market share in 16 of the past 17 years.

Countering Geico's Gecko is Progressive's Flo, who since debuting in 2008, has helped lure nearly 2.5 million fans to the insurer's Facebook site. Today we've got Allstate's Mayhem, Farmer's University and State Farm's magically appearing agents. You may cringe at the suggestion that there are lessons to be learned here, but you can't argue with their results.

Am I suggesting that your engineering firm should start using a talking lizard to promote your services? Absolutely not! But I am suggesting that the principles that other, more marketing-savvy industries have learned over the past century could contain some very valuable lessons for us newbies.

Is it time for engineering to become sexy? Maybe. It's certainly time for us to move to the bright side of the road by learning what geniuses like Warren Buffet already know.

CAPTURING THE VALUE OF 'FREE'

I love getting free stuff. The feeling of walking away (legally!) with something that you haven't had to pay for is right up there with sunshine and blue skies.

There's free stuff everywhere you look: Coke is on sale at the grocery store: buy one get one free. Stay one week at the Turtle Dove Resort, get a free rental car. Buy a new BMW, get free oil changes for life.

It's interesting to note, however, that you rarely get something for free unless you've paid for something else. Try telling the grocery store that you only need one bottle of Coke, so you'll take the free one please. Hardly ever does anyone hand you something of value and say, 'It's yours!' without you first having paid for something else.

So let's decide that 'Free' simply means it isn't a line item on your bill. You paid for it, but it just didn't show up on the invoice.

As we think further about the notion of 'free' it's easy to see there are two kinds. The 'random act of kindness' sort of free only scores points if it's done anonymously. In our relentless efforts to make it to heaven, we've all been taught to do good deeds, but to do them quietly, without taking credit—you'll be rewarded later. The 'good for marketing' kind of free, however, scores no points if no one knows about it. If you give your client something for nothing and they aren't aware of it, you don't get any goodwill credit.

What's all this got to do with your engineering or design firm?

You give away stuff for free all the time. Project scopes that stretch into size XXL without corresponding fees, the advice you give away without compensation, the extra time you spend with your clients. All these represent your equivalent of 'buy one, get one free.' To make matters worse, your clients come to expect all the free stuff without having to pay.

29

Let's learn how to give away free stuff while enjoying the marketing benefits AND maintaining control.

When you write your next contract, include a clause that says something to the effect of, "This fee includes up to $2,000 of additional scope items that are not yet identified, at no additional charge." Then, when the client asks you for something that's outside the scope, remind them of their 'free' scope expansion and happily do the task. When the $2,000 (or whatever amount is right) runs out, let them know they've had their free bottle of Coke and they'll have to pay for the next one.

Any time you do provide a service at no charge, memorialize it with an invoice. Create an invoice that documents the work done, the hours taken and the fee for services. Then take a red pen, cross out the bottom line, write "No Charge" in big red letters and mail it to the client. They'll be thrilled at the great customer service and the free stuff. But they'll also catch on that you're monitoring the creeping scope. You'll get the goodwill points while building in a reluctance to let the scope expand into size XXL.

YOUTUBE WINS!

I've shared with you before some of the wisdom that I enjoy so much from Roy H. Williams, one of the great advertising geniuses of our time. He recently offered some thoughts about social media and how effective it can be in promoting our businesses. Here are Roy's (paraphrased) thoughts compiled from some recent blog entries.

Facebook, for business, is a mirage. Can it successfully gather a crowd to hear a band perform at a bar? Absolutely. Social media, social event. Can it successfully be used by a physically-existing retail or service business as a substitute for mass media? No. It cannot.

A physically-existing business is one that lives in the land of sunlight. A purely online business, by contrast, lives in the light of the plasma screen. Check into those Facebook success stories and you'll find them all to be businesses that sprang into existence after 2003. I defy you to find a physically-existing business who enjoyed success prior to 2003 that is now reducing its mass media budget because it has found Facebook to be a more effective use of ad dollars.

The answer is YouTube, not Facebook. YouTube is a message delivery vehicle that has yet to be maximized and its potential to grow a business is vastly greater than Facebook. The number of search strings typed into YouTube each day is second only to Google.

There were 1.46 trillion YouTube views in 2012. Let's put that in perspective: One million seconds is about 12 days. One billion seconds is nearly 32 years. One trillion seconds is 31,688 years. This means 46,264 people per second click to watch a YouTube video 24/7/365. Nearly 3 million per minute, 4 billion per day. That's 13 times the population of the United States every day.

And not all those YouTube views are just a bunch of teenagers watching a hundred videos a day. While it's true that YouTube reaches 67% of the US population 18-34, it also reaches 59% of the 35-49

31

population, 52% of the 50-64 population and 48% of the 65+ population. Want to see a video on how to do something? Install a sink? Rig a block and tackle? Change a filter? Type it into YouTube and a self-appointed expert will appear. What does your firm know that you'd be willing to share for free in exchange for worldwide recognition?

There is no "next big thing" on the media horizon. I see only a teeming host of small and medium things. Here's one of the best of the medium things. Get a smartphone. Use it to collect video of customers giving you real-world, real-time testimonials "in the moment." Post these testimonials on YouTube and embed them on your website. It's free. You don't even need to know what you're doing. Professional video editors are plentiful and affordable in the cloud.

You have things to say. Why not say them to the world? Why bother to fight against the wind on Facebook? The opportunity is on YouTube.

Thanks, Roy! You can find more of Roy's wisdom at his website http://www.rhw.com/

SLAM DUNK ON A WHITEBOARD

My client informed me over the phone that, with just a few days' notice, they'd just been asked to interview for a major project. "Can you please come and help us prepare?" So here we were in their boardroom at 8:30 on a Saturday morning with the hoped-for client showing up for the interview first thing Tuesday.

My client had in mind to assemble a glorious PowerPoint event that began by tracing the history of their company, moved into a discussion of the many other projects they'd done like this one, marched through the project team's top-notch experience and closed with a promise to exceed the client's expectations.

So far it sounded like every other presentation from every other design firm, so I asked them to set their ideas aside for a moment and switch hats. I invited them to pretend they were the client with all his worries and concerns and then to tell me about the project. It took them a moment to get into the 'role playing' mode, but I soon heard an interesting story.

Turns out the client had already hired another architect to do the project and they'd made some progress. But it came to a screeching halt when the lead consultant had a heart attack and was laid up in the hospital. Under tremendous time pressure, the client was forced to find a replacement. (I didn't bother to point out that not one thing they were planning to say in their interview would address the client's obvious question: "Can you get it done on time?")

When I asked if they could meet the tight schedule, they mumbled something about putting their best team on it. So I thought it was time to focus on the 'how' of getting this time-crunched job done before the deadline.

The room had whiteboards lining two walls and I asked their project manager to take notes as we brainstormed. Over the next three hours we filled four whiteboards with notes, schedules, critical decision points, work flow charts and more than a few wild and crazy ideas on how to get this sucker completed on time. By noon we had concluded that, if they followed the aggressive work plan, the project could be completed four weeks early.

By this time it was noon. They said it was great that we had worked out the schedule, but "when were we going to start working on the presentation?" I replied, "We're done! Let's have some lunch, then I can catch an early flight and get home." The look of shock on their faces told me I would have to explain a little more.

"Look," I said, "this client is lying awake nights, frantic that he won't be able to meet his obligation. He already knows you've got the skills to do the work, that's why you're on the short list. The only thing he wants to know is whether you can get it done on time. You've just proven you can, so what else is there to present? We've just spent three hours of hard work figuring out a solution to his problem. There is sweat dripping from those notes! You're going to walk out now and not come back until Tuesday morning. Then you'll go over these notes and show him how the project will be done." I then went a step further and said, "If you do it like this, I guarantee you will win this project."

When I spoke to them after the interview they could hardly contain themselves as they related what happened. As they went through the notes on the boards, the client madly took notes and asked questions. Once, when they pointed out a crucial meeting date, he said, "I think I've got a conflict on that date. Would it hurt us to move it back by one day?"

When they finished, he handed them the project on the spot and offered them a fee that was about 20% higher than they'd intended to ask for. Then he sat for the next half hour and ridiculed the other firms he'd interviewed. "They talked about the history of their firms, showed me projects they'd done before and introduced their teams to me. But you showed me how we're going to get it done!"

Moral: Nothing is more important than the view from behind your client's eyeballs.

RESEARCHING DOWN THE LADDER

When you read through that RFP that just landed on your desk it will usually name a contact person who has been designated to dispense only the information that the client feels consultants require. Your challenge is that this contact person will only ever give you the 'official' answers and will also make sure that all your competitors are given the answers to the insightful questions you ask. Something about keeping the playing field level...

But I'm all for tipping the playing field as far in your favor as you can. Yes, I DO want to create an unfair advantage for you!

One of the tricks is to find a back door into the organization that will allow you to gain important insights into the agency or organization (and perhaps even the project) that aren't influenced by the 'company line.' An effective way to do this is to go down in the organization and speak with someone at the operations level. Someone, preferably, without a title, who isn't shy about telling you what's really going on. Previously, I told the story of buying coffee for a harried transit hub supervisor and learning more about the issues facing the project in 20 minutes than I had in the previous two weeks.

Why not take the janitor to lunch? No one has ever done that before and he'll be so shocked and thrilled that he'll be happy to tell you anything you want to know. You'd be surprised at the number of conversations the janitor overhears and how much he knows about what is and isn't working. This back door approach will likely provide you with insight that you'll never get when dealing with the gatekeepers.

Another effective way of building these lower-level connections is to have your technical staff communicate with the technical staff of the client's organization. They have a professional camaraderie that can cross corporate lines and give you a vital link to critical information.

Be careful not to abuse your new insider best friend, though.

Expecting too much might be risky for both of you. Treat them with respect and gratitude and you'll be happy together for a long time to come.

BLOOD SUGAR

You've been there. You're sitting in what ought to be an interesting presentation and feel your eyes getting heavy. Then heavier. You close them for what you promise will only be a second and then wake up suddenly as your head jerks forward to your chest. You open your eyes wide, shake your head a couple of times and refocus your attention on the speaker as she drones on.

And what if you are that presenter, watching as heads nod and eyelids droop? What can you do to improve the situation?

For those nodding off in your audience who are genuinely sleep-deprived, don't worry. They've got that peaceful easy feeling and you should let them snooze. For the rest, you can design your presentation to make it easier for them to pay attention.

First consider the time of day when your presentation will be given. At 9 AM we're all fresh and clear. We've had a good night's sleep and our morning coffee and we're ready to pay attention. But picture that audience at 2:30 in the afternoon. The blood sugar is falling, the brain is counting the hours to the end of the day, lunch is still digesting and a short nap sounds like the best thing going.

If your presentation is early in the day, you can ask more of your audience. You can give more detail, assume a higher level of concentration and provide fewer mental breaks. But if you're on right after lunch, you should lighten the tone a little. Do this by shortening the time you spend talking about each topic. Change things up regularly between speaking, focusing on visuals and getting the audience involved. You might want to introduce a discussion portion or have samples that you can pass around for the audience to feel and hold.

How about a little enthusiasm and dynamism in your delivery? Get excited about your topic and let it show. If your monotone makes it seem as if the one falling asleep is you, why shouldn't they fall asleep too?

Walk around, change your location, if possible, walk into the space where the audience is. Take off your jacket, roll up your sleeves, give them something different to look at. Change your voice too. Lower and raise the pitch, volume and speed of delivery. A long silent pause, followed by a few rapid-fire sentences, will get everyone paying attention again.

It's the long stretches of sameness that encourage us to drift off. What can you do to introduce contrast and change? In addition to changing up the internal dynamics of the presentation itself, I've been known to bring and pass around chocolate chip cookies during an afternoon presentation. In one critical sales presentation that was scheduled for 4:30 on a summer afternoon, I even brought cold beer! Of course that's not going to be appropriate for every audience, but in that particular case it was much appreciated and completely consumed!

When you design your next presentation, think about the time of day, your audience and the state of their blood sugar. Then do them a big favor and make it easier to stay awake.

CAREER LIMITING OBSTACLES

Your favorite pro football team has a problem. Their best place kicker—the guy with the 87% lifetime average—has retired. The scouts are working overtime, scouring every college and high school football and soccer team in the country, looking for THE ONE who will replace the legend.

The head coach's phone rings and one of the scouts is calling from somewhere in the Midwest. He's found the perfect guy—right height, right weight, amazing kicking record, great concentration under pressure, incredible accuracy. He's the real deal!

There's just one, teensy, tiny problem… A month ago he was in a terrible car accident and now has only one leg. Other than that, he's perfect!

Let's switch focus. You're a Project Manager. You graduated with top honors from the best engineering school. You can design and build anything. You're organized, efficient and productive. You're hot stuff!

There's just one, teensy, tiny problem… You really don't like doing business development. You're uncomfortable meeting people, you don't do small talk and you can't remember names. Or maybe you actually CAN do all those things, but you just don't like to.

I see and hear it all the time. And the excuses that are given are legendary. "It's just not my personality." "I'm not really a people person." "I'm much better working on projects." "I'm yer typical engineer! (chuckle, chuckle)"

We live in a wonderfully inclusive society. And thank goodness for that. We go to great efforts to ensure that there are as few barriers as possible to anyone who wants to achieve their dreams, no matter what their disadvantage or disability. And more power to the one who works hard to overcome whatever obstacles life has set in front of them.

I apologize if I'm seeming to be insensitive, but there are some limitations that we simply have to recognize as career limiting obstacles. A Project Manager who can't or won't actively engage in business development, who can't or won't bring in enough business to at least feed himself and his team is a non-starter. About as much good as a one-legged placekicker.

EVERYBODY has to make some contribution to the get-work process. And Project Managers are at the front line of that effort. The good news is that, even if you don't rate yourself as a natural business developer, you can learn to be. Yes, it will take some effort and likely some practice that will push you out of your comfort zone. But Dale Carnegie, Toastmasters and the Self-Help and Business sections of any bookstore have enough resources to turn you into a machine for selling. There are no excuses.

Somebody has to say it out loud, so I will:
If you can't or won't play an active and successful role in business development, you're not qualified to be a Project Manager. You might be a fabulous engineer, and we need lots of those. But if you have the title of Project Manager and aren't actively bringing in a steady supply of work from both existing and new clients, you aren't doing your job. Any questions?

THREE ROADS TO TRUST

In the A/E/C business there are three distinct models that are used in business development. None of them are perfect and each has its own set of advantages and disadvantages.

Before we start, let's review our definition of 'business development.' It's the proactive development of one-to-one relationships between two people who want to do business together. This means that you're getting to know someone at a deeper, more personal level because you both know that a trust-based relationship is critical if your work together is to be something more than a simple transaction.

The first model is the 'Rainmaker.' This is the full-time, professional salesperson whose job is to scour the landscape looking for and closing deals on projects. He or she doesn't get involved in executing the project once it's been landed because they're back out looking for the next. The advantage of the Rainmaker is that he or she is selected based on, and is devoted full time to, sales ability. The downside is that there must inevitably be a hand-off to the people who are going to deliver the project and the clients may not like that.

Then there is the Door-Opener. This is an individual who has close connections in your target market and can get your firm in the back door to meet the key decision makers. Very often engineering firms will hire a retired State DOT employee or military person who can walk right back into their old office and start introducing you to their friends. (Who says you can't go home?) The advantage is that you get to live in the halo of their ready-made relationships. They also usually know the ropes regarding procurement rules and regulations and can help steer you through that maze. The disadvantage, once again, is that eventually there will need to be a hand-off to the project delivery team.

The third, and by far the most common model is the Seller-Doer. We also call this the Eat-What-You-Kill model as it requires the Project

Manager to find enough work to keep herself and her team supplied with work. The upside of this model is that the all-important relationship begins with the person who will be responsible for delivering the project and no hand-off is required. The downside is the inevitable feast-or-famine waves of too much, then not enough work as you struggle with the conflict between nurturing your relationships and getting your work done. It also puts business development in the hands of people who are frequently poorly skilled at it and just as frequently don't like it.

Which model is the best? Business development is a team sport and you need every one of these people playing on your side. The Rainmaker needs the project delivery team, the Project Manager needs someone to scan the horizon for opportunities and we all need friends who can get us in the door.

There are also some guidelines for using each of the three. The Rainmaker and Door Opener tend to be best used in the search for new clients in new areas of opportunity. The Seller-Doer tends to be best used to ensure a steady supply of repeat work from existing clients. These aren't hard-and-fast rules, and there's no reason the Rainmaker can't be talking to current clients or the Seller-Doer turning over new rocks. But you want to make the highest and best use of your business development resources and that arrangement tends to produce the best results.

HOW TO BE LIKED

Harry Connick, Jr., along with a number of other big name stars, starred in a holiday season movie—*Angels Sing*—that should be added to everyone's holiday movie list. Chandler Canterbury, who was 14 when the movie was filmed, plays his son, David.

HC Jr. tells how he and Chandler were hanging out between scenes "when he looked at me and said, 'What's the secret of being popular? How do you get people to like you?' "

What a great question! And an even better question for those involved in business development.

Harry's answer? "The secret of being liked is to always ask five questions before you say anything about yourself. People won't remember what you said about yourself, but they'll always remember what you asked about them."

This is fabulous advice that we all need to practice every day. And if you doubt it's true, try this simple experiment. The next time you're at a social gathering—a neighborhood party or a business reception will do—walk up to someone you don't know, introduce yourself, and then begin talking about yourself. Tell them about your job, your family, last summer's vacation, your hobbies, your favorite sports teams and your pet turtle, Ralph. As you're talking about yourself, keep track of the time and see how long it takes until your new 'friend' finds an excuse to end the conversation and move on to someone more interesting than you.

Then move on to part two of the experiment. Find another person you don't know, introduce yourself and begin asking them questions about themselves. Ask about their job, what they enjoy most about it, what they find the most challenging. Ask where they went to college and how their school's football or basketball team is doing. Ask how they like to spend their leisure time. With each of these questions, be very sincere, pay close attention and ask follow-up questions whenever you can. Keep an eye on how long this conversation goes on. You'll find that everyone else has gone home but you're still having a great conversation with your new best friend. Why? Because you spent the whole time talking about her favorite subject—herself. You shifted the conversation to put her at the center of the universe.

Where is the center of the universe? It's right there where you happen to be right now, just like it is with everyone. The first and most important rule of business development etiquette is to put your client at the center of the universe and focus on his or her favorite subject.

You were born with two ears, two eyes and one mouth and, as your mother said, you're intended to use them in that proportion. There is far too much valuable information that we miss when we're talking. Let the other person talk. When you talk, use your time to ask questions. Lots of sincere questions that not only get you more information, but show that you're genuinely interested. If you can't wait for the other person to finish speaking so that you can get your two cents in, you're missing a huge opportunity to build a high-quality relationship and learn some valuable information. Next time you're in a conversation, take five minutes to listen, observe and keep quiet.

SHOW YOUR WARTS

We all know them. They're the sorts who, after they've dropped the ball, go to great lengths to assure us it wasn't their fault and deflect the blame to some other poor schmuck. The saddest thing about this kind of person is the utter transparency of their efforts. Usually, the fault is so obvious that their efforts to duck responsibility would be humorous if they weren't so despicable.

The one thing we all have in common with this poor sap is that we screw up. Regularly. And sometimes in a really big way. What separates us is what we do after we step in the doo-doo.

Who would you rather work with: The person who makes a mistake, then tells you why it wasn't really a mistake, why it doesn't matter and why it actually wasn't their fault? Or the person who comes to you, tells you they've made a mistake (often before you find out on your own) and tells you what they're going to do to fix it? Your clients would rather work with that person too.

When you try to hide a problem you've created or deflect the blame elsewhere, the trust that others have in you disappears. But when you step up and face the music, your credibility takes a huge leap. "If she's being honest with me about this, I've got to believe she's going to be honest with me about everything." It doesn't feel very good in the moment, but the long-term benefits are enormous.

Sure it's embarrassing to screw up. We all want to appear to be perfect and our egos take a big hit when we fall short of the mark. Our first instinct is to hide and hope no one notices. But then, when someone does notice, our second instinct is to make excuses or point the finger elsewhere. Every one of these actions simply digs the hole deeper, making it that much harder to climb out in the end. As much as it goes against your survival instincts, resist the temptation to duck, cover up or deflect. It makes you look like the two-year old who covers his eyes and thinks that nobody can see him.

Your clients know you're not infallible. They know you're going to make mistakes.

When you make that inevitable mistake, that's the time to show what you're really made of. Step up right away, tell the truth about what happened, then tell what you're going to do about it. It isn't that you screwed up. It's about what you do after it hits the fan.

When you mess up, 'fess up. This is a golden opportunity to set yourself truly apart from everyone else.

HOW MANY PEOPLE KNOW YOU?

I don't mean how many LinkedIn connections or Twitter followers you have. That's too easy. I mean, how many genuine prospects, key decision makers and potential clients are aware of your firm, know about its capabilities and would be positively predisposed to consider you for a future project?

In other words, how far does your brand reach?

Many firms are extremely well known by their clients. They've spent years developing a strong and loyal following from a small segment of the market. And those clients have served them well with a long record of repeat work and a steady supply of projects.

Far too many firms, however, are virtually invisible outside that limited group of clients. I see it all the time in my travels around the country. A firm has built up tremendous loyalty from a relatively small number of clients, but they've done little or nothing to establish a presence in the larger market. Brand recognition is extremely high among those they work with. But it's almost non-existent outside that small circle.

This didn't used to be a problem. A reasonably sized collection of clients could keep a firm going for years, if not decades. In just the past few months however, I've had five different CEOs tell me that things have changed. Where they used to be able to depend on the phone ringing regularly (in many cases that has been the entire marketing plan), they can no longer count on that. In these times of tight money and sequestered budgets, client loyalty is fast becoming a thing of the past. "We'd love to work with you again but we simply have to put this out to competitive bidding. We owe it to our (shareholders) (taxpayers) (boss) to make sure we're getting the best possible deal." They're not the same old client that they used to be.

In this environment you can choose between two strategies. The first is to lower your costs, lower your fees and lowball the price on every project you chase. You WILL get work. Probably lots of it. But you'll struggle to make money, you'll have high staff turnover and your clients will run the minute somebody else comes along with a fee that's five cents lower than yours.

The second is to adopt an aggressive branding strategy. To spread your reputation much farther and much wider than simply your client list. The smart firm has learned to stop chasing projects and start chasing clients. The really wise firm sets its sights on owning the market.

In the past 10 years the concept of brand has moved into the AE world in a big way. Prior to that, branding was a notion that applied to soap and soup and cars. In today's connected world, however, your strong brand lets you become the 'must-have' firm in your market. Despite their tight budgets, today's clients still have the ability to work with the firms they choose. And they are choosing to work with those firms that have great reputations, are well-known and well-respected across a broad swath of the market.

Responding to RFPs and consistent delivery of high quality projects with great customer service is absolutely vital in building your brand. But your strongest competitors do that all day long. Today's strong brand has to be supported by aggressive, broadly-cast communication across the entire market, not just to your client list.

Aggressive brand strategies worked well for soap and soup and cars. Now it's your turn.

THERE ARE NO NEW CLIENTS

I recently happened to view an old photograph from the mid-1800's showing a group of pioneers trundling across the prairies in their covered wagons. So many green fields to claim! So much open space!

Not so much today. The 'green field' project is the exception as we work to recycle the old ones.

The same is true with clients. When it comes to growing your firm, there are no new clients. Every client out there today is currently being served by someone else. Now, whether they're being well-served or not is another question. But you simply won't find a client who isn't already being served by one of your competitors.

That means that every new client you gain will have to be won away from an opponent. And that makes things a lot tougher. In any competition, the incumbent always has the advantage. Just ask any politician. The one who's there first has already won once, they're the proverbial 'devil you know' and they have habit and inertia on their side.

Your job to unseat them is a double challenge: Not only must you persuade the client to hire you, you have to persuade them to let the previous consultant go.

What does this mean for your marketing efforts? It means you can't win on your merits alone. It means there's no holding back and you have to win by clearly demonstrating the overwhelming advantage of working with you.

Your entire win strategy must focus on those things that differentiate you from the competition. Let's face it—your list of past projects is just like theirs. So in addition to talking about your experience you're going to have to show what they'll get by working with you that they won't get from the other guy.

The best way to unseat an incumbent is to overwhelm the client with such an impressive effort that they'll wonder why they ever hired the other guy in the first place. You're going to need:

- A top-notch proposal with a huge 'WOW!' factor. That means professional-grade graphic design, writing and packaging
- Lots and lots and lots of client testimonials
- Engaging, exciting and well-written success stories. Not those boring 'challenge-solution' sleepers and certainly not a collection of lists
- A presentation that's so well-choreographed and polished it could be a Broadway show
- A clear demonstration of service that's so far above the average that it sets its own new standard

The client wants to know what they're going to get from you that they aren't getting now. And it has to be worth the effort of switching. They won't be willing to switch, if they're simply going to end up with the same or even just slightly better skills, experience and service they have now. Your argument has to be unique, compelling and enthusiastic.

How will you make their effort to switch worthwhile?

AN ACCESSIBLE WRITING STYLE

David Ogilvy, often considered the father of modern advertising, was responsible for a revolution in how companies communicated with their customers through their marketing.

"I don't know the rules of grammar. . . . If you're trying to persuade people to do something, or buy something, it seems to me you should use their language, the language they use every day, the language in which they think. We try to write in the vernacular."

David Ogilvy

Since your primary goal in a proposal (or any of your marketing) is to persuade a client, then you need to use all the tools at our disposal to accomplish that goal. One of the most important is to make the content of your proposal easily accessible and understood. Too many technical professionals have been trained in technical writing and use that style in their proposals.

Sure, technical writing may be accurate, but it's hang-me-now-please! boring to read. You want to generate excitement and enthusiasm in your reader and that doesn't happen from perusing something that reads like a specification.

Instead, try writing in a more comfortable, easy-going style. One of the tests you can use to check your writing is to read a passage that you've written out loud to yourself. Then ask, "Does this sound like me talking?" If it sounds a little (or a lot!) too stiff and formal, rewrite it and relax your writing style. At the risk of sounding like a TA in a creative writing course, here's a sample of "before" and "after" proposals, where the style has become much more relaxed and easier to read.

Before: Accurate, yet crushingly dull

Preconstruction Services
During the preconstruction phase Acme Construction shall:
- Develop detailed estimates of costs of materials, equipment and labor
- Review facility life cycle costing implications
- Conduct value analysis and value engineering
- Conduct a constructability review
- Review and finalize schedule
- Assemble and coordinate Bid Packages
- Identify and prequalify subcontractors and suppliers

After: Far more interesting and engaging, yet still accurate

During preconstruction we will:
- Estimate the detailed costs of materials, equipment and labor. Then we have to live and die with our estimates.
- Examine the total cost of ownership that you'll incur with your facility to ensure a small savings now doesn't become a maintenance nightmare later.
- Conduct a detailed value analysis to make sure the materials and equipment specified are those that give you the best value for your construction dollar.
- Walk through the entire construction process to uncover any constructability challenges and solve them now before the pricey crane is brought on site.
- Review the schedule to find the fastest possible way to get this facility completed and your revenue flowing.
- Assemble the individual bid packages to ensure 100% coverage but avoid costly overlaps, confusion and wasted time and money.
- Identify and prequalify those subcontractors and suppliers who are best suited to contribute to the success of this project.

With the consequences of getting it wrong so critical, it will be reassuring for you to have Acme Construction's experienced Preconstruction Team, with our wealth of knowledge and lessons-learned, assembling the framework for a successful project.

If you've spent your entire career writing technical reports, this might, at first, seem a little too casual for you. But relaxing your writing style makes it so much easier for your clients to understand and retain your message. And isn't that the first step in persuasion?

MEASURING YOUR MARKETING SUCCESS

We've all learned some tough fiscal lessons over the past few years. One of them is that we need to constantly ask if we're getting a good return on our various investments. In the marketing arena, firm owners are asking hard questions about the spending of scarce dollars in the effort to win new work. And so they should! As much as we marketers might squirm under the spotlight, the questions are legitimate and need to be asked and answered. If spending can't be justified with a clear return it should be redirected.

That said, marketing ROI is a slippery pig to grab hold of since it's hard to assign clear credit to any particular undertaking. That new client may have first heard of your firm from an award you won, then learned more about you through your email blast program, been impressed as one of your team members spoke at a conference, then made the final decision when your well-written proposal was competitively priced. While each of these initiatives contributed, it's impossible to allocate precise percentages of effort that resulted in the win.

There's an old saying in the ad business: "Fifty percent of all advertising works. We just don't know which half." While I know more than a few engineers whose hair might catch on fire from this notion, there are some very clear guidelines that will help you get the most from your marketing dollars and useful ways to measure your return.

Here are the four measures that I like to use:

1. Do you have a marketing plan and is it being executed on schedule? If you have a solid marketing plan and it's being rolled out relatively close to schedule, you WILL see results from your efforts. The results will vary and come from different

sources that are too diverse to be worth the effort to track individually. Think of it like a fitness program—if you're eating properly and exercising daily, you are getting more fit, whether you weigh yourself every day or not.

2. Is 'brand awareness' increasing as measured by client surveys? The best client survey device I know of comes from a company in North Carolina called Design Facilitator. www.designfacilitator.com I have no problem blatantly plugging a product that works well and I highly recommend it.

3. Are you receiving positive, informal feedback? Your senior executives, project managers and business developers ought to be seeking regular feedback from clients in their day-to-day engagements. A simple, 'How are we doing lately?' or 'Is there anything we could be doing to improve our service to you?' at every encounter will give you plenty of informal feedback. Don't worry too much about recording this feedback, but talk about it regularly and take it seriously.

4. Are your hit rates increasing? This includes click rates on your web site and win rates on your proposals and interviews. These should be tracked carefully and you ought to be seeing steady and regular improvement.

There you have it—four areas to measure and only two of them produce actual numbers. (Sorry, all you left-brainers, sometimes the world isn't quite as calibrated as we'd like.) But I firmly believe that these will produce all the measurement you need. Beyond that, any tracking efforts are more trouble than they're worth. Spend your time and resources on the effort of marketing and the score-keeping will be easy.

FIND THE SWEET SPOT

Dear Engineering Abby:
My firm has provided the same services for the past eight years and the quality of our work has continually gone up. Yet our ability to charge reasonable fees has continually gone down. What's going on and what can I do about it?
Tired in Toledo

Dear Tired:
Welcome to the free market economy at work! When you first started selling your services, you were a new name in your market with a new twist on how your services were delivered. You appeared to be different and your ability to charge a higher fee depended on your clients' perception that they were getting something of greater value than they would from your competitors. Over time, the differences between you and your competition, both real and perceived, has gradually disappeared. When a client can't find a meaningful difference between the services they get from you and those they get from other firms they select on the basis of low price. This drives your fees down. Even as incremental improvements are made, such as the use of technology or improved quality, most competitors keep pace with these upgrades. Client expectations go up but the price continues to go down.

In this situation you have three choices. The first and least effective is to reduce your costs in order to remain profitable at the same prices. Witness the airlines eliminating in-flight meals and negotiating wage concessions from their workers. This is a downward spiral that can only end in a sudden crash.

The second is the hardest—offer services that no one else is offering or deliver them in a way that no one else is. This is the 'niche market' strategy and it's increasingly difficult to find an unoccupied niche.

The third, which is also challenging but can be very effective, is to find the sweet spot in both your services and your clients and milk them for all you can.

This strategy has two components. Step one is to review all the services you offer and identify those that have the lowest return on your investment—i.e., the services that involve the most work for the least profit. Stop selling the lowest 20%. Let some other firm lose money there.

Step two is to identify those services and clients from which your return is the highest. There is no doubt a small number of clients and services that continually provide you a higher profit than normal. Study these clients and services. Analyze what it is about them that allows you to make higher margins. Sit down with those clients and ask for honest feedback about your firm. Why do they like working with your firm? What do they value the most?

When you feel you've distilled the high value services and clients, focus your efforts on these areas alone. What else do those clients need that you can offer? How can you expand the list of clients buying the high-value services? Don't be afraid to expand into services or joint ventures that those clients need but might seem non-traditional to you—that's where the high-profit firms are making their money today. Financial services, program management, commissioning, hyper-track project delivery systems, risk management consulting, are all examples of specialty services offered by high value engineering firms today.

Don't be afraid to conclude that your current staff mix can't keep up with the changes. The same people doing the same thing is what has turned your service into a commodity. Change is tough, but failing to change is deadly. While we love to celebrate the free enterprise system, we also have to live with its tougher side. Your firm must constantly evolve and grow if you are to stay on the bright side of the competitive road.

STOP SELLING ENGINEERING!

The AE profession is a mature industry that offers little to distinguish between suppliers. In short, traditional design services, sold in a traditional manner are a commodity. End of discussion.

This leaves us with three choices:

1.   Gripe.

The commoditization of A/E services is old news, yet many firms stick their heads in the sand and complain while they wait for things to get back to "normal." News flash: This IS normal.

2.   Enroll in the 'Sam Walton School of Business.'

The selling of commodities is a viable and popular business model. You just need to reduce costs and sell in high volume. You can so this, but not with your current organization. You'll need service menus with fixed prices, ultra-high productivity, rigid scope control, and aggressive pricing of extras. Instead of an A/E firm, you'd run a hyper-efficient 'project factory.' It might not appeal to you, but if well-managed you'd make slim margins on each sale and high dollars from the volume.

3.   Stop selling engineering.

But you're not actually getting out of the business; you're simply going to modify how you're doing business. You'll shift the focus and re-package the services you already provide. You'll still provide engineering, but the focus of your sales and the value you provide to clients will shift to new areas. If you're adventurous enough to pick this option, you're again left with three choices:

Option #1:   Differentiate!

The foundation of all marketing is differentiation and you MUST be able to definitively show your clients what it is that sets you apart. Today's tradition-bound design professions offer little to distinguish one firm from another. Websites spout the identical rhetoric and proposals are a head-butting contest, pitting your list of projects against theirs, with nobody emerging a winner.

It's time to learn from the experts. Watch a few ads on TV for car insurance, banks and cellular service providers—all commodity services—and see how they distinguish themselves. It's rarely by saying that they're actually better at their core business than the other guy. (They've realized that's impossible.) Instead they focus on being seen as faster, smarter, cheaper, prettier, sportier, hipper, sexier, funnier, more understanding, up-to-date or attentive. Think this can't apply to engineering? Think again.

Option #2:   Show me the money!

Traditional A/E services offer a standard group of project phases: schematic design, design development, contract documentation, bidding, and construction observation. These are so standardized there are precise fee percentages assigned to each in most contracts.

Over the last 30 years entrepreneurial firms have turned this to their advantage. Early on we saw the emergence of Construction Management firms who tore the back end off traditional services and charged big fees to clients frustrated by poor on-site performance. Then another group used big-picture thinking to package the upfront phases into the 'new' service of Program Management. Clients gladly signed on at high prices. Still more enterprising firms have combined the Internet with low offshore labor costs to drive down the cost of document production.

In each case they've turned their back on the traditional approach, built their offerings around highly profitable, specialized offerings and left tradition-bound firms holding high liability and low fees.

Option #3:   Stellar Service.

Have you ever walked into a store and, three minutes later, walked back out having decided you'll never set foot in that establishment again? How about the opposite? Where you walk out two hours later with a big pile of merchandise for which you paid a premium, but you've also decided that you'll never shop anywhere else again. How did you arrive at those decisions?

What's it like to shop in your engineering or architecture store? Do you offer a customer 'concierge,' available to address any need your clients may have? Most real estate agencies now offer this convenience. Do you provide 24/7 access? You can't find a business-oriented travel agent that doesn't. Does your firm offer real-time, web-based project updates? All banks provide round-the-clock access to critical data. Do you provide money-back guarantees? It's hard to find a business today that doesn't. Does your firm provide mandatory, on-going training to all your staff in customer service? Disney World sets the standard for this. All the hotel chains provide it to their employees and even the grocery stores are learning the importance.

Any one of these items would dramatically set your firm apart from your competition.

Each of these options requires a commitment to and embracing of dramatic change that hasn't shown itself in the A/E industry yet. This is a profession that likes things the way they've been. Who will be the first to step up to the plate and stop selling engineering?

"Nothing stops an organization faster than people who believe that the way they worked yesterday is the best way to work tomorrow."

Jon Madonna
Former Chairman and CEO,
KPMG International

But we've never done it like that before!

Anonymous Engineer

LUNCH WITH THE MAYOR

A few weeks back I was visiting with a client and heard an interesting story. His firm provides a variety of engineering services to small municipalities throughout the state. They've got a great history and reputation and do pretty well for themselves. But they don't have their foot in every door and those towns where they aren't the engineer of choice give them a little competitive heartburn.

This one particular burg has been working with a different engineering firm for some time now. But, like good business developers should, my guys called on the mayor and the key town council members regularly anyway. They've been keeping the embers glowing by staying in touch and letting the relationship grow.

Over the last few months they learned that not all was well between the town and its incumbent engineer. In fact, Hizzoner the Mayor was getting more than a little ticked at what he felt was less than stellar customer service and was losing patience with them. So quietly, without disparaging anyone, they spent a little more time in the town than they might have normally.

Then, a couple of weeks ago, the current engineer calls the mayor. Says he has to postpone a meeting. Again.

"That's it!", says Mr. Mayor. "I've had enough." He called my guys that afternoon and when I last spoke to them, they were scheduled to have a nice, friendly lunch with the town's key decision-maker.

Lessons to be learned:
1. Your clients are NOT committed to you for life. They're around until they decide they don't want to be anymore.
2. Business development never stops.

3. Pay attention! Ask your clients how things are going. Ask if there is anything you can do to improve your service. Never assume that all is well.

4. Waiting for the next RFP to come out so you can stampede in with all the other buffalo is a strategy for losers.

5. The little things really DO matter.

6. Just because they went to the dance with somebody else this time, doesn't mean they won't go to the dance with you next. Keep asking.

7. Taking your clients for granted is a sure way to reduce your backlog.

8. Your next new client is currently being served by one of your competitors. What are you going to do about it?

A few pages back, I wrote about the fact that there are no new clients. That should serve as both a warning and an incentive. May the most deserving firm win!

IS YOUR MARKETING DEPARTMENT
A TRUSTED ADVISOR?

So many firms aspire to 'trusted advisor' status with their clients. And so they should. A trust-based relationship speaks clearly to the value that you bring.

One of the hallmarks of this kind of rapport is that you regularly show your clients opportunities and possibilities that they may not have seen themselves. You bring them more than they expect to receive. It's the very definition of 'added value.'

What about the relationship between your firm and your Marketing Department?

In way too many instances, I see the marketing staff operating as a glorified secretarial pool. Proposal writing is an exercise in cut-and-paste and 'Save As.' Technical staff have the first and last say as proposals are edited and presentations are prepared, and the management team—with their engineering credentials—dictates what makes for good marketing.

This all-too-common approach misses out on an enormous opportunity and ignores the same kind of enlightened value that we try to sell to our clients.

If you've been smart in your hiring, the marketing team members who spend their days trying to help you win more work know a thing or two about marketing. They have at least a little (and sometimes a lot of) training and knowledge in marketing theory, writing, editing, graphic design and the vital art of persuasion. Yet far too many firms fail to take advantage of this great resource.

While it's true that you know your clients and their preferences best, it's not always true that you know the best way to communicate the value you can bring to them. There is an entire knowledge base and skill set that the vast majority of firm owners and technical staff simply don't possess. When your Marketing Department serves in that trusted advisor capacity, the collaboration between your knowledge of the client and their knowledge and skills in marketing produce results that are far beyond your ability to achieve on your own.

Now, if you're a member of the marketing team and are smugly reading this, don't think that you're free of responsibility. One of the major reasons that firms don't treat their marketing staff as trusted advisors is because they've not been shown any reason for that trust.

When I took over as VP of Sales and Marketing for a $300-million construction company, I inherited a marketing staff of seven people. They had great skills in writing, graphic design, editing and marketing theory. But they didn't know squat about construction. How could I expect the head of the healthcare construction group to trust one of my team to write a great proposal for the next hospital project?

Within a week of my arrival, the entire team had been outfitted with hard hats and steel-toed boots, and we made regular outings to the construction sites. They learned about pile-driving equipment, the subtle art of the concrete pour and the life-and-death importance of controlling dust when you're renovating a neo-natal intensive care unit. I gave small workshops on writing and editing and we critiqued each other's work. They participated in the monthly Superintendent meetings (at 5 AM!) and built great friendships with the foremen and workers.

The proposals improved dramatically.

We also organized a program to teach the technical staff about marketing. We held lunch-and-learns, sent around a newsletter and generally went out of our way to inform the rest of the company about what we were doing, why we were doing it and how marketing works.

Within six months the entire relationship between the marketing department and the rest of the company had been transformed. They began to believe that we could represent them in far better ways than they ever could have done for themselves and we treated them as our best customers. We had become trusted advisors.

HOW TO LEVERAGE SECOND PLACE

You're the first of the losers. You won on the wrong day. You're too good for this game.

No matter how you candy-coat it, some other firm won the project and you didn't. What do you do now?

The most common response to coming second is to pick yourself up, dust yourself off, and move on to the next RFP. But that strategy will miss out on a number of opportunities to leverage your First-Runner-Up status. Rather than licking your wounds, think about these options:

Conduct an internal debrief

While the proposal effort is fresh in everyone's memory, have a quick conversation about what went well and where you dropped the ball. Did you follow your standard procedures for proposal development? Did everyone meet their responsibilities on time? Was the document the best you're capable of producing? In retrospect, was it really a project that you should have pursued? Are there lessons-learned that can be applied on the next effort?

Conduct a debrief with the client

Whether you win or lose, always ask the client for a debrief on your proposal. It builds a stronger relationship, raises the quality of future proposals and drives up the odds of winning in the next round. But ask the right questions. Asking, "Why didn't we win?" will give you useless answers such as, "Yours was one of many good proposals," "It was a tough decision," "Please continue to submit," etc. Instead, give your client permission to be constructively critical. Ask specific questions that invite real feedback:

- Tell me the three things you liked most about our proposal.
- Tell me the three things you liked least about it.

- What would you like to see changed that might increase our chances of winning next time?

Ask to review the winning proposal

In most public sector selections (and many in the private sector too, if you just ask) the client is either happy or obliged to show you the other submissions. Review them with an objective eye. Was the winning proposal easier or more engaging to read than yours? More attractively designed? Did it address issues that you neglected? If you combine your review with your client debrief you can also ask:

- What did the winning firm include in their proposal that put them over the top?
- What are the common traits that have made recent winning proposals stand out from the rest?

Protest

Robert Heinlein was an American science fiction writer who famously said, *"Never try to teach a pig to sing; it wastes your time and it annoys the pig."* Much the same can be said for protesting the results of a selection process. While the procurement rules in many public sector arenas allow you to protest, I've never seen this course of action end well. Of course, if you feel that a serious injustice or malfeasance has been committed, you should act. But even if you succeed in getting a change in the outcome, you won't have made any friends.

Ask for another project

This is a particularly smart idea. If you were shortlisted and the choice between your firm and the winner was close, ask the client to share the wealth and award you another one of their projects. Most clients have an ongoing program that requires a steady stream of design services. If you impressed them enough to make the decision tough, ask if you can show your stuff on another project. While it's an unusual approach, I've seen it work and it ought to become more common.

Stay in touch (and wait for the winner to trip)

One construction company I know came second on a major hospital renovation. After a year of preconstruction the winner started into the project. In week one on the job they cut a major power line, flooded part of the intensive care unit and thoroughly annoyed the chief hospital administrator. In week two the second place team was called in to take over from the firm that had just been fired.

Relax

Projects are like buses—there's another one coming along in about five minutes. You will never have a 100% hit rate and there are some factors that you simply can't control. After you've held your debriefs, reviewed the winning efforts and reinforced your relationship for the future, take a deep breath, go home, hug your kids and relax. Tomorrow's another day.

THE NEED BEHIND THE NEED

I'm a big believe in unfair advantage. No level playing fields for me, thanks—I'd much rather head into a contest with everything tilted in my favor. I highly recommend this approach any time you chase after a project too. You need to give yourself all the unfair advantage that's available.

The best way to tip the table in your direction is to have more information than the other guys. You accomplish this by collecting as much information about the client, the project, the selection process, the competition, and the surrounding circumstances as possible.

Information harvesting never stops—you're doing it as you build relationships, reading the paper, listening to or watching the local news, having casual conversations and, of course, as you cruise the Internet. Every bit of information you can get your hands on is valuable. It's the key to success in sales and the more you have, the stronger your position.

As you amass information, you want to be looking as much for the intangible things as you are for the 'hard' information. Yes, find out about schedules, budgets, scopes of work and technical specifications. But you also want to learn about personalities, political winds that might be blowing, hidden agendas, alliances and all the other behind-the-scenes insight you can gather.

This is what we might call 'the need behind the need.' Imagine, for example, that you're going to respond to a civil engineering RFP that calls for the installation of a bicycle lane along Pacific Avenue, from Elm Street to Main. While the technical scope is straightforward, if you didn't also know that this project is part of a re-election bid by the Mayor who feels he hasn't connected with the 'green' segment of the town, you'd miss a significant, if unspoken, element in the selection process.

Another example—the industrial client, looking to expand a

manufacturing facility. Knowing that your client is being threatened by an encroaching competitor and wants to get a new product to market as fast as possible to help preserve their competitive edge, is likely going to affect how you write your proposal and choreograph your interview.

This doesn't have to take much time. I once spent about five minutes on a Google search that yielded a small but vital fact about a client. That information, which had nothing to do with the scope of the project, ended up playing a huge role in our team winning the project.

I'm a big fan of what I like to call, 'walking-around knowledge': those tidbits of information that don't seem relevant when you first hear them. But if you hold onto them, they become puzzle pieces that snap together to form a clear picture of what's going on behind the scenes.

The more you know about your client and their project, the better your chances of winning. So the next time you're having lunch, playing golf or just riding an elevator with anyone, follow the advice your mother gave you: You were born with two ears and one mouth and you're intended to use them in that proportion. Listen. Ask a probing question, then shut up and listen to the answer. You never know, you just might gain an insight that will help you win that next big project.

IT'S ALL ABOUT BREAKFAST

I was having dinner with a valued client a while back. We'd both had a couple of glasses of wine and he was pontificating on all manner of interesting topics. When we eventually got around to the subject of business development he stopped, looked me in the eye, and said, "David, it's all about breakfast!"

I didn't have a clue what he was talking about so I asked him to go on.

"Breakfast meetings are where all the ideas are born," he said. Then he went on. "If you're there when the first idea is sketched on the napkin, you're going to be there when the last brick is laid. So make sure you have breakfast with a client, a decision-maker or a key influencer every morning."

This guy is one of the most naturally gifted business developers I've ever met. He grew his firm from nothing to Holy Cow! in a very short time and here he was sharing one of the secrets of his success. I was paying attention!

Every good business developer knows that sharing a meal is a great way to get to know someone on a more personal level. There's just something about 'breaking bread' together that lowers inhibitions and removes obstacles. I think the act of eating – something we all have to do – highlights the common denominator in us all and lets us see the opportunities for connection, rather than the reasons to keep our distance. Whatever the psychology, if you're a business developer, you like company with your mealtimes.

But of three meals in the day, he was recommending breakfast as the best one for business development. Does it have to do with sunrise, new beginnings, fresh energy? Who knows! But it's worked for him in spades and I'm not going to argue with success. How many times each week do you have breakfast with a client?

I've always encouraged firm Principals, business developers and Project Managers to make a habit of taking clients to lunch. In fact, I like to suggest a quota: Principals and business developers should share a meal with a client five times each week. Project Managers should set the goal at twice a week. We eat 21 meals each week and as many as 90 each month so those are small percentages for the return we can get.

Of 21 meals each week, my friend makes sure he shares 15 – 18 with clients, decision makers and influencers. That's a high bar but it's paid off for him. Who are you seeing for breakfast this week?

WHAT'S IN YOUR PROPOSAL?

Your proposal is not just a technical document conveying data. It has to persuade, assure, convince, comfort, and win over a client who is about to put a great deal of money and trust in your hands. A proposal is not only about qualifications. It's a personal message.

To be sure, clients aren't much help when it comes to rethinking how we write and structure our proposals. They've been stuck in the same ruts, for just as long as we have. The RFPs they send out reinforce our old habits of submitting cold, lifeless data in list after list that simply confirm how much we look just like our competitors.

Here is an excerpt from an actual RFP issued by a municipal client looking to retain design services. It describes what the City would like to see in the proposal responses.

The proposal shall include:
1. *Size and make-up of the firm.*
2. *Names and resumes of personnel to be assigned to the project.*
3. *A list of related projects and references.*
4. *A list of other disciplines that would be included in the proposal.*
5. *Previous experience with similar projects.*
6. *Proven ability to adhere to schedules and budgets, within particular emphasis on design consulting.*
7. *A description of the methodology and procedures to be used for the total scope of this project. (i.e., concept phase, design phase, public input phases).*
8. *Fees disbursement and hourly charge-out rates for the concept design phase.*

Taken at face value, this becomes a handy checklist that can be given to a Marketing Coordinator, assembled and submitted to the client for review. It would be filled with boilerplate and generic answers that are copied and pasted from the answers given in previous proposals to other clients.

But this would entirely miss the point!

Instead of taking a checklist approach to your proposal, you need to crawl inside the client's head and discover what it is they are actually looking for. Instead of taking a checklist approach, read the list above again and realize that what the client really meant to say was:

The proposal shall include:
Sufficient information, presented in a concise, easy-to-access and persuasive manner that will conclusively show the selection committee why yours is the only firm on the face of this planet that should even be considered for this project.

If the RFP were written in that way, you might think twice about the mind-numbing lists that make up the bulk of your submissions.

Contrary to commonly held beliefs, and in order to 'hot wire' your firm to your client's brain, you must think in terms of there being only three sections in a good proposal:

1. First Impressions—in which you grab the client's attention and draw her into an interesting and engaging document.
2. What We're Going To Do For You—in which you relate the services you're about to provide and how the client's world will be so much better for having worked with you.
3. Who We Are—in which you demonstrate that your firm is an exact match with that imaginary firm they'd love to hire, if only it existed.

Of course you can't think of these three categories as you would normal sections separated by tabbed dividers. Instead, think of them as three critical messages that have to be delivered to your client— sometimes subliminally.

These three sections will be intermingled through the proposal because they client will likely have specified the tabbed sections you're to include. As you write, recast the standard, traditional proposal sections into this new context. At all times, imagine yourself as the client, having to review and evaluate the proposal. Is your writing style interesting and engaging? Is your fit for this project obvious? Do the photos and illustrations you've chosen complement the message and add understanding and clarity?

Clients in this business are as bad at writing RFPs as we are at writing proposals. And they use the same techniques—'Save As' and cut-and-paste. When you're preparing your next submittal, don't ignore the client's instructions, but go beyond the checklist and give them a proposal response they didn't expect.

WRINKLE-FREE SHIRTS

Why would you buy:

- A car with traction control?
- Wrinkle-free shirts?
- A dishwasher with a five-year warranty?
- A painless dentist?

You don't buy them for those features. Instead, you buy them for the peace of mind when driving in slippery conditions, the freedom from ironing while traveling, the assurance of reliability and the anxiety-free experience of keeping your teeth healthy.

Not long ago I was working to help a construction company fine tune its marketing message. We spent some time brainstorming about features that the company had to offer its clients. Here are some of the items we came up with:

- Safety record
- Awards
- Track record
- Volume of work
- Great people
- Systems and procedures
- Community involvement

We then went through an exercise to translate each of these features into key benefits that will accrue directly to their clients.

The company's safety record becomes the clients'
- Lower insurance costs
- Reduced project costs
- Avoidance of bad PR
- Happy workers
- Peace of mind

The company's awards become the clients'
- Prestige and recognition
- Comfort
- Reduced risk

The company's track record becomes the clients'
- Reduced risk
- Increased likelihood of on time/budget
- Reduced time demands
- Better decision-making

The company's volume of work becomes the clients'
- Reduced costs through buying power
- Increased speed through leverage on subcontractors

The company's great people become the clients'
- Pampered attention
- Ease of communication
- Extended network
- Access to important information

The company's systems and procedures become the clients'
- Trust
- Reduced risk
- Comfort
- Ability to focus on other priorities

The company's community involvement becomes the clients'
- Extended network
- Prestige
- Link to additional opportunities

I believe you get the point. Your customers and prospects don't care about the features of your company – the year it was founded, its six offices in four states, and the state-of-the-art technology you use. They only care about the benefits that will accrue to them and how much better their life will be after choosing you. So focus on the benefits and leave the discussion of features to your came-in-second competitor.

REALLY BAD PHOTOS

A picture is worth 1,000 words. But those words will say nasty things about your firm if you don't choose and use your images wisely.

I can't count the number of times I've seen photos included in proposals, presentations, on websites and even in printed brochures that are just plain awful. Heavily pixilated, out of focus and boring are the most common offenses. But there are other transgressions that border on the criminally dumb too.

Low resolution photos

Even the least expensive cell phone today can capture a digital image that is capable of being blown up to billboard proportions. So why do I see so many photos that look more like an ancient Greek mosaic? If the digital image isn't large enough to blow up without pixilation, don't use it. Take it again at a higher resolution or find another.

Poorly composed photos

There are a few simple rules of visual composition that anyone can learn in about three minutes. Have good visual balance, don't cut off important elements of your image, find an angle that lets the light enhance the subject in the best way. Google 'how to take a good photo' and share the information around the office.

Boring photos

There is nothing the least bit engaging about a photo of a piece of PVC pipe lying in the bottom of a muddy trench. But that's what I encounter when I look at the project experience sheets from countless civil engineering firms. The other disciplines have their own versions of these predictable pics. Yes, it might be a photo of the project, but there's a reason we end up burying this stuff—it's not nice to look at! We put the pipe there for the benefit it brings: Clean water from a tap. So let's have a photo of a cute three-year old enjoying a glass of cold water on a hot summer day.

Photos without people

The architects are the worst offenders on this one. It always seems that we wait until 5 AM on a Sunday to take the photo to make sure there isn't a living, breathing sentient being within five miles of the project! I know there are rules about signing waivers for people in photos, but get the staff from your office or hire your cousin to sit on the bench. The project was designed to accommodate humans—let's see a few populating it!

Photos without captions

Flip through any magazine and you'll see that every photo has a caption. That's because we are too busy (or lazy) to read the articles. So we look at the pictures and read the captions. The client reviewing your proposal is no different. And don't have the caption simply say, "New 14-inch watermain along Main Street." Instead, let them tell a story: "Smith and Jones worked hard to keep the business owners along Main Street informed and up-to-date as the new watermain project progressed."

If you don't have compelling and engaging photos of the project, use some high quality, life-style photos that show people living the great life that your infrastructure project helps support. Or mix and match some life-style photos in with your more technical shots. There are many great stock photography websites that have high quality, royalty-free images at really low prices. Try istockphoto.com or fotolia.com.

Poor quality photos in your marketing and business development efforts look unprofessional, amateurish and cheesy—not traits that make clients want to rush to hire your firm.

RUNNIN' WITH THE BIG DOGS

I think I'm going to coin a new phrase: "Leadership Marketing." It means having the guts and the audacity to recognize that conventional marketing wisdom in the AE world makes you, well, conventional. And if your firm aspires to be extraordinary, to set itself apart from the conforming crowd, you need to practice Leadership Marketing.

If the truth be told, there's a lot of mediocre marketing going on out there. And there's a really good chance that your firm is wholeheartedly participating. What does mediocre marketing get you? Mediocre response from clients, mediocre fees, and a plaque in the Commodity Hall of Fame.

Mediocre marketing consists of doing what you and everybody else have been doing for a long time. Websites look the same, proposals look and read the same, and presentations are pretty much interchangeable with the exception of your company logo on the slides.

Leadership Marketing shakes it all up. It uses unconventional ideas and steals flagrantly from the leading marketing ideas outside the AE business. It tosses conventional wisdom on its head and generates loads of buzz. It gets people talking about your firm, it raises your profile and it makes your clients and future prospects sit up and take notice.

But it takes courage for firm leadership to admit they don't have all the answers. And to admit that sometimes, the way we've been doing it simply got us to where we are today. If we want to get to somewhere else, we'd better embrace some new ideas.

One of the hallmarks of Leadership Marketing is that it doesn't look to competitors in the same business for inspiration. We've learned pretty much everything there is to learn from other firms in the design professions. The next lessons have to come from outside our industry.

In a previous section I cited some bar-raising examples that other service-based industries have now accepted as standard operating procedure:

- The customer concierge offered by most real estate agencies to address any need their clients might have.
- The 24/7 access to customer support offered by most travel agencies.
- The real-time, online access to critical data and services that banks have been providing for years now.
- The mandatory, continuous staff training in customer service that hotels, resorts, retail stores, banks, airlines and countless others have embraced.

Are you ready to adopt any of these stand-out-from-the-crowd strategies?

Marketing has become a key performance function in today's engineering firm. Without a high-performing marketing team—whether that team is one person or 20—that pushes you, kicking and screaming into the future, your firm simply cannot compete in the mainstream.

After all the work you've done to refine productivity, quality control and project management, isn't it time to turn your attention to the function that feeds the firm?

It's simply unrealistic today to think that your firm can successfully stand out against the crowd by touting your technical prowess and your ability to deliver a project on time and within budget. If you want to run with the big dogs you need a marketing machine that keeps you ahead of the pack.

Adopting a 'Leadership Marketing' approach will give you the guts and the audacity to be extraordinary and to set your firm apart from the conforming crowd.

THE STRAWBERRY JAM THEORY

Marketing resources are like strawberry jam—the farther you spread them, the thinner they get. And if you're anything like me, a thin, barely visible skim of jam on your toast just won't cut it.

One of the most pervasive challenges I see among marketing folks around the country is the tendency to spread themselves too thin. Proposal writing, brand building, press releases, business development coordination… Oh, and can you please speak to this person asking for a donation for the local high school booster club? That's marketing, isn't it?

If it seems too often that you're only barely managing to stay a step ahead of the freight train that's bearing down on you, it might be worthwhile to rethink your approach. Operating in reactive mode all the time gives you no opportunity to plan, strategize or reflect on where you've been or are heading.

So is the solution to have more jam or less toast? We all work with a finite supply of resources— time, money, staff—but there are ways to leverage the resources you do have to make them more effective. Here are some tips I've found useful:

Prioritize
Take a look at your marketing plan. (You have one, right?) Then ask yourself, "What's the ONE THING I could be spending my time on that will take us to those objectives the fastest?" When you've identified it, set aside at least 50% of your time to devote to this task. Everything else is secondary and can wait. If you don't have a marketing plan, maybe preparing one is your ONE THING.

Focus
We often spend more time switching between tasks than we do working

on the tasks themselves. Instead of launching a Facebook page, an internal newsletter, a PR campaign and an update of your resume library, pick just one. A really good job done on just one of those efforts will bring you far more benefit than a poor or half-finished job on all four.

Outsource

While you're the only one who can do certain marketing and business development tasks, there are many that can be done by freelance experts on a contract basis. Market research, development of your contact list, graphic design, template building, writing, editing and staff training are just some of the functions that can be easily, effectively and economically outsourced.

Interns

While I'm vigorously opposed to the current practice of getting student interns to work for free, I'm a big fan of bringing in these energetic, enthusiastic and low-cost staffers to work on one-time projects. With just a little coaching and management, they're naturals for organizing your photo library, researching that new market you've been contemplating, updating resumes or tackling that huge pile of yet-to-be-filed proposals.

Each of these tactics will make your jam go a little farther while still retaining that sweet strawberry taste.

If you're not a jam fan, here's another way to think about it: Imagine that you're an Army General heading into a battle with 5,000 troops. Would you string your soldiers out in a line, 5,000 men long and one man deep and say, 'Charge!?' Of course not. It would be suicide.

Instead you'd concentrate your troops and focus on a small number of key targets. Once that high ground was secured, you'd regroup and then aim for the next strategic objectives.

If you're going to execute a marketing strategy, make the effort worthwhile. You'll get far more benefit from one really well-executed initiative than from five ideas that are only half-baked.

SMOKE AND MIRRORS

There's a dirty little secret that we marketers don't want the rest of you to know. But I'm feeling rather generous so I'm going to let you in on it: Marketing is dead simple. There is nothing complicated about it at all. It's far less complex and difficult than engineering or architecture. It's much simpler than construction. Plus, it's easy to learn and easy to execute.

There, I've let the cat out of the bag.

If it's that simple, why do so many firms struggle with marketing? Part of the problem is that we marketers have a vested interest in you believing that this is a mystical world of smoke and mirrors, governed by obscure incantations or the fickle finger of luck. We'd like you believe that without us, you're sunk.

Another significant reason is that we were lied to. I went through architecture school where they told us, with straight faces no less, that if we simply did our work well, everything else would take care of itself. Who needs to know about marketing when we're so good at what we do?! Simple or not, they certainly didn't offer any training in marketing.

Finally, many firms believe that they can soldier their way to marketing success with brute force instead of knowledge. "If we simply respond to enough RFPs we're bound to win our share and be successful." This approach ignores the simple rules of marketing and relies on hope that you are selected from an ever-expanding list of worthy competitors. As the wise man said, "Hope is not a strategy."

Rather than a mysterious black box, marketing success consists of knowing and following a few basic rules. If you know and follow them it works. And it works every time. If you don't know and don't follow them, you get mixed results, unpredictability and a really low return on your marketing investment.

There are just three rules of marketing.

1. What makes you special? What sets you apart from your competitors? What do you have that can't be found on just any street corner? What will I get from you that I can't get from anybody else? What do you have that I'd be willing to pay a premium for? If you can answer this question confidently, authoritatively and convincingly, you're well on your way to marketing success. If you can't, welcome to Commodity World!

2. What's in it for me? Everybody in the world has the same favorite subject—themselves. Your marketing message has to recognize and respond to that truth. Don't tell me that you've been in business since 1958. Instead, tell me that I'll benefit from almost six decades of continuous lessons-learned. Don't tell me that you've done 28 projects for other clients. Tell me that the experience you've gained will be applied to the unique challenges of my project. Don't tell me how good you are. Tell me how great my world is going to be when we're working together.

3. Over and over and over again. This is the easiest rule of all, but the one that's least understood and most frequently broken. What adjectives come to mind when you hear the word Nike? Apple? Disney? McDonalds? BMW? Over time, these brands have actually purchased a small piece of your mental real estate. That name recognition builds up a credibility and an equity that translates directly into sales and profits. What adjectives does your target market (note that I don't say 'clients') think of when your firm's name is mentioned? The long-term buildup of brand recognition is a fundamental requirement for successful marketing and requires consistency, regularity and patience. Those firms looking for in an instant return on effort lose interest and respond to another RFP.

Marketing is not an enigmatic black box, requiring a secret handshake and decoder ring. It's a series of simple, logical steps, taken in order and applied consistently for a predictable outcome. It doesn't make up stories, exaggerate or engage in any smoke-and-mirrors deception. When marketing is done well it simply shines a light on the reality of what you do.

But it shines a really bright light. It makes a lot of noise so that people notice and pay attention. Marketing, done well, educates, engages and excites your clients, your prospects and your entire target market. It connects with them over a long period of time so that you, too, own a small piece of their mental real estate.

Marketing is not smoke and mirrors. But nor is it simply responding to an endless parade of RFPs.

THE SALES PREVENTION DEPARTMENT

There is a department in your firm whose job is to prevent sales, deter growth and undermine prosperity. There is no sign on its door and it doesn't have a box in the org chart, but it's there nonetheless.

With the best of intentions, this department swings quickly into gear when the economy is tight, competition is tough and revenues are down. It usually works under the guise of 'Overhead Reduction' but its net effect is to prevent further sales and avoid winning more projects.

When revenues are down there is a natural and correct inclination to reduce overhead costs. Focus on revenue-producing activities and cut back on spending that isn't related to accomplishing fee-paying work. Usually the first function that's cut is marketing. And I'll never understand why.

If the temperature in your house is freezing, do you turn off the furnace? If you are choking and can't breathe, do you ask the paramedics to cut off your oxygen supply?

Marketing is the function that brings in work. It's your lifeline and your food supply. Why on earth would anyone think it's smart to cut back further on the very thing that we need the most?

In an effort to shine a light on this insanity, I've offered alternatives: Get rid of the office space. Lay off the accounting staff. Turn off the lights and unplug the phones. In response I hear patronizing chuckles and a litany of reasons why we can't survive without those vital resources.

But there's a universal truth that I've adopted as the tagline for my own company and it's very applicable here: "Nothing happens till somebody sells something." Without a steady supply of profitable work your office space, accounting team, lights, phones, computers and even your valuable staff are nothing but overhead.

My favorite children's fairy tale is *The Emperor's New Clothes*. You remember this one: It's about two penniless shysters who come into town and promise the Emperor a new suit of clothes made of a special cloth that is only visible to the best, the brightest and the most worthy. No one, including the Emperor, wants to admit that they can't see anything so the con continues. When the Emperor parades his new clothes before his subjects, it's a naïve little boy who finally points out the obvious: Yon King is nothin' but naked!

I find that frequently, conventional wisdom isn't very wise. This is one of those cases. When money tightens up, the best performing firms INCREASE their investment in marketing. They cut back in other areas, they borrow, they reach into shareholder's pockets, but they recognize that marketing and sales is not dispensable overhead, it's a critical investment that will get them out of the hole they've fallen into.

In many regions and markets we're still crawling slowly out of the longest-lasting recession in any of our memories. Many firms are still holding the purse strings very tightly and marketing is almost nowhere to be seen. If this is your situation, step back and look at the situation. Does it make sense to you, or is the Emperor just naked?

TIMES CHANGE. DEAL WITH IT.

In some ways it's like watching your grandfather contemplate the latest smartphone. He kind of shakes his head, mutters something about back-in-the-day and gets a wistful look in his eye as he realizes that his time has come and gone.

Here's the version of that story I hear almost daily, accompanied by the same melancholy look:

"We had projects walking in the door for decades with almost no marketing effort."
"Our reputation was all we ever needed."
"Our founder and CEO brings in all the work. Everybody loves him! He's retiring next year."
"Our clients are treating engineering as a commodity."
"None of our engineers like to sell."

Nostalgia and sentimentality are nice around the holidays, but they won't bring profitable work in your door. Sure, it was fun while it lasted. But the recession dealt a body blow to the design industry, which was already on the ropes before it hit. This is the new normal of today and any firm that does not step up to the challenge of this new economic reality will go the way of your grandfather's hand-cranked phone.

Marketing—non-stop, over-the-top, aggressive and intelligent marketing—is an absolute necessity. And that doesn't mean simply cranking up the number of RFPs you respond to. That gets you nothing but a lower hit rate. It means embracing a marketing and sales culture, engaging marketing professionals and learning as much about marketing as you know about engineering or architecture.

Here are four non-negotiable must-do's:

1. Differentiate! Find something—anything!—that sets your firm apart from the crowd. Clients treat engineering as a commodity because all the firms providing it look and sound and act EXACTLY the same. I don't care if you become known as the firm that drives around in pink trucks, so long as you do something to set yourself apart.

2. Build your brand! Within the design professions, branding is the least understood, least utilized and yet most powerful marketing tool available. The day in which you can say that it only works for soft drinks and soap and discount car insurance is over. Yes, it works wonderfully for them. And the same principles can work for you too. Learn about the power of branding. Then leverage it to your advantage.

3. Write fewer proposals. But make them intelligent, clever and laser-targeted. It's long since been proven that throwing lots of proposals out there is a really bad way to win work. It costs a lot of money, it frustrates your marketing coordinators no end, and it simply doesn't work.

4. Get serious about business development. And get comfortable with an unpopular four-letter word: SELL! Yes, design professionals have to sell, sell regularly and sell hard. Selling requires a set of skills that wasn't taught in engineering school and you need to learn, practice and hone those skills daily. The founding CEO can't and won't do it forever.

Your grandfather will manage just fine without a smartphone. But you have no choice when it comes to embracing a marketing and sales culture if you want to survive and even thrive in this game.

MARKETING IS A PROCESS, NOT AN EVENT

There've been countless occasions over the years when I've been invited to sit in on a business development meeting. Most firms have them—that weekly gathering around the spreadsheet when we run down the list of project opportunities, assess the status, the likelihood and the desirability of each and ensure that someone is judiciously following up.

And each time I'm witness to one of these meetings I'm reminded of the huge disconnect between most firms' marketing plans and their business development activities.

Marketing plans almost invariably state that "we want to chase clients, not projects." I wholeheartedly agree. Building a long-term, multi-connection relationship with a client organization that can provide a steady supply of profitable work over the years is a really good idea. It allows you to build a book of business that isn't based on competitive bidding.

But when the rubber hits the road, the vast majority of business development activity is spent searching for and responding to RFPs along with every other firm on the horizon. Is your firm guilty? If your BD meetings focus on a list of project opportunities, many of which have already had a proposal number assigned, you're guilty.

The truth is that, despite their commendable strategic statements, the marketing plans of most firms are centered on chasing projects, not clients.

This exposes the large gap that exists in most firm's marketing plans. They start with a broad, strategic statement such as, "We're going to position ourselves as the preferred engineering provider in the widget market," but then make a magical jump to "How do we win the XYZ project for the Acme Corp.?"

How do you bridge that gap? A friend of mine, who is the Director of Business Development & Marketing of a good-sized firm, is reminding everyone in his company about the importance of the sales funnel.

I'm sure you've seen this metaphor: The wide mouth of the funnel is where you're prospecting, building relationships with qualified client organizations, learning about their needs and preferences and letting them get to know the advantages of a working relationship with you. At this point there isn't an RFP in sight.

Further into the funnel, things start to narrow. There are fewer prospects but the ones who remain have been filtered to ensure that their needs and culture form a good fit with your capabilities and approach. Still no RFPs but the promise of future work is bright.

At the narrow neck of the funnel, relationships have evolved into specific opportunities and the best few of those have been identified. Proposals are generated and delivered and the negotiation and closing process begins.

Believe it or not, I still encounter way too many instances of firms that have their marketing coordinators combing the papers and the online sites for RFP announcements. Announcements by clients they've never met for projects they haven't seen coming.

Business development is not an event. It's a process. A process in which you carefully choose partners based on mutually complimentary goals and attitudes. A process in which you get to know each other before you get serious. A process through which you make it much more likely that this is going to be a long and fruitful relationship.

As Humphrey Bogart says in the closing scene of Casablanca, "Louis, I think this is the beginning of a beautiful friendship".

BRANDING ISN'T SUPPOSED TO WIN PROJECTS

You're breezing along the highway at 75 miles an hour when, out of the corner of your eye, you glimpse a flash of bright red and white. The images seem vaguely familiar and, though you might not actually look, your subconscious registers the colors and shapes of Coca Cola. Then, in an instant, your attention goes back to the jerk in the Camry who's self-righteously doing barely the limit in the passing lane.

What just happened? You were exposed to a brand-building moment and without your permission or even conscious awareness, it worked.

Branding is the most powerful marketing tool available to you. It has the power to position your firm as the preferred provider in your market, build loyalty, attract sole-source inquiries and significantly lower your costs of winning work.

Yet almost no one in the AE business has embraced it. Why not? Because a branding campaign will not win a project.

When Coke puts a billboard on the side of the highway they have zero expectation that you'll see it and immediately pull off at the next exit to buy a can of their sugar water. They do expect though, that you, along with every one of the carefully-counted 318,435 drivers who pass that sign every day, will have the Coke brand brought back to the front of your mind and have that logo, those colors and that name burned even more deeply into your grey matter. Then, on a later occasion, when someone asks if you'd like a soft drink, you're more likely to say, "Sure, I'll have a Coke!" simply because that oh-so-familiar word will fall out of your mouth before any other.

A branding strategy isn't intended to sell Cokes, Camry's or engineering projects. Instead, it's intended to 'condition the targeted market to be positively predisposed' (in marketing-speak) to consider such a purchase when the time comes to buy.

Branding has three objectives, the first of which is to establish name recognition. They can't hire you if they don't know you exist. Introducing you once isn't enough. Real name recognition, the kind that takes hold and really sticks, takes place over a long period of time after many repetitions. How many times in your life do you suppose you've heard or seen the words "Coca Cola?"

The second objective is to enhance reputation. While it's good to know the Coke name, potential customers also need to know what it stands for. Branding repeats and reinforces the message with every 'touch'— "15 minutes can save you 15%"; "The ultimate driving machine"; "Just do it".

The third objective is to establish what marketers like to call 'mind share.' Geico, BMW and Nike all own a little piece of your mental real estate. They've invested in it over a long period of time with thousands of tiny little touches through advertising, public relations, social media and all the tools in the brand-building kit. Mind share is the phenomenon that allows you to see a green lizard and think "Save 15%", or an apple with a missing bite and think "Cool."

Branding is a numbers game. It's not about talking to just your existing clients or the prospects you're following for projects. It involves talking to your entire market. That means that ANYONE who might ever want or need your services throughout your entire geographic reach needs to hear or see your message. So these broadly cast messages need communication techniques that have a low 'cost-per-touch.' A business development technique such as taking one client to lunch could cost you $150 per touch. Sending a weekly email blog like this one to 45,000 prospects costs 0.17 cents per touch.

Years ago I was working with an engineer and suggested that a direct mail program would be a good idea for his firm. He instantly nixed the idea with a dismissive, "That doesn't work! I sent out 50 letters one time and didn't get a single project from it."

Fifty letters, one time, isn't a branding effort. It's a waste of paper and postage. Nor was it supposed to win a project. But 1,000 postcards or emails, once a month for a year… That's a great start to a branding program.

ARE YOU A TONGUE-TIED BUSINESS DEVELOPER?

If you're anything like 88% of the adult population you would identify yourself as being somewhat shy in social settings. Walking into a meet-and-greet social, or attending a networking reception is right up there with a root canal on your list of favorite things to do. But if you have any responsibility for business development (and you do!) the ability to make conversation is pretty important.

Susan RoAne is a best selling author who wrote one of the most practical, useful and down-to-earth books for the terminally modest you'll ever find. Titled, "How To Work A Room," it teaches you exactly that. She identifies a series of cultural roadblocks that conspire to keep us hiding behind a plant and then provides really useful advice for getting around them.

The first barrier came from your mother when she taught you not to talk to strangers. That made tremendous sense when you were walking home from school at seven years of age. But it's lousy advice when you're working a trade show or mingling at a conference reception. What to do?

RoAne suggests that we redefine the term 'Stranger.' A stranger is someone you don't know and with whom you have nothing in common. But at a meeting of professional colleagues you're not with strangers at all. Even though you may not have met before, you have a lot in common with the others attendees, the first thing being attendance at the same event. Since common ground is the starting point for any relationship, spend a moment before you walk in thinking about what you have in common with the other attendees. It will help you feel more comfortable and give you some conversational cues to help break the ice.

The second roadblock is the admonition to wait to be properly introduced. That's also good advice when you're 12 and in a roomful of adults. But at the meet-and-greet, if you wait to be introduced you're going to be awfully lonely.

RoAne's advice is to prepare and practice a self-introduction that is clear, interesting and well-delivered. Tailor it to the event, whether social or professional, and include something about yourself that establishes what you have in common with the others there. Less than tens seconds is enough to give the essential information and perhaps something interesting about yourself that may engage people in conversation.

Your mother is guilty of this third barrier too! She told you not to be pushy—that good things come to those who wait. Well, there's pushy and then there's pushy. The fact is that, in a networking situation, waiting for someone to find and introduce you is an exercise in futility.

To overcome your anti-pushy training, RoAne suggests that you shift from 'guest' behavior to 'host' behavior. A 'guest' waits for someone to take their coat, offer them a drink and introduce them around the room. But a 'host' is concerned with the comfort of others and actively contributes to that comfort by meeting people, introducing others, starting conversations and making sure their needs are met. If you adopt the 'host' behavior, you have a job to do at the event. You have responsibilities and an excuse to be as outgoing as you need. If you make the meeting your event you feel more comfortable extending yourself because it's your job and others will be naturally drawn to you.

Networking in social settings doesn't come easy to most of us but it's a critical skill for anyone involved in business development. Get yourself a copy of Susan RoAne's fabulous book and become a Master Schmoozer.

CLIENTS WANT YOU TO BE A COMMODITY

Have you ever had to fill out and submit one of those wonderful SF 330 forms that the federal government loves so much? Ever completed an SF254 or 255? If you have, you're complicit in the effort to turn you into a commodity.

Those are pretty harsh and even inflammatory words, but let's step back and take a harsh look.

In force since 1972, the Brooks Act is a law requiring federal government agencies (and many states and other public agencies have adopted the process) to select AE firms "on the basis of demonstrated competence and qualification" rather than by price. In essence, the Brooks Act established qualification-based selection.

And then the fun began.

If you take price (a very handy and empirical variable) out of the equation, you're left with a hodge-podge of touchy-feely, soft issues that are seriously challenging to sort through. My firm has done 27 projects like this one. Your firm has only done 24. Can anyone truly say that my firm is more qualified? At some indistinguishable point, we're both fully qualified. (Don't get me wrong—I'm not advocating price as a basis of selection. Read on.)

With qualifications-based selection, the challenge became, how to select the 'most' qualified firm from among a healthy list of 'fully' qualified firms. The selection criteria quickly become intangible and highly subjective. This leaves public servants, who have to answer for their decision-making, in an uncomfortable spot.

How to rationalize the intangible?

Introduced in 1975, the Standard Forms 254 and 255 were intended to level the playing field and let a broader spectrum of AE firms compete for government work. But, as with all changes, there were unintended consequences. By reducing qualifications to what amounts to a spreadsheet, firms could be lined up, measured and ranked. Once ranked, the top few would be asked to submit a price and the winner announced. The real value that a firm could bring to the project was frequently lost in translation.

Things have evolved since 1975. Today, the number of fully qualified firms for any given project is huge. The truly incompetent weed themselves out pretty quickly and those that are left are all more than capable of executing the project on time, within budget and to the required standard of quality. As a profession, you're pretty darn good at what you do!

Recognizing this, and in an effort to make the process more streamlined, the SF330 was introduced in 2004 but it still lines the firms up, then measures and ranks them based on what is hoped will be rational criteria. In other words, the goal is to compare apples to apples, whether you're an apple, an orange or a cumquat.

Your marketing and business development efforts have the opposite goal. You want to stand apart from the crowd, proudly individual and incomparable to any other firm that attempts to stand beside you.

Read most firms' SF 330's and you'll fall asleep. The project descriptions simply say, "We were present." They don't say, "We saved the project from disaster," or "We contributed a brilliant idea," or even "We screwed up royally!" They simply say, "We were there."

So fight back! Don't write boring project descriptions, write intriguing stories. Don't include predictable photos, use compelling, thought-provoking images. If you have to use the silly form, make it sing and shout!

I once helped a design firm win a large federal government project by introducing a brand new section to the SF Form. Titled, "Special Introductory Section," we took three pages to tell the firm's story in a way that was compelling, engaging and persuasive. Yes, we took a chance that some Contracting Officer would reject it as "Non-responsive," but we counted on his or her innate curiosity and made it to the short list.

It's the job of the public sector contracting officer and the private sector procurement department alike to devalue what you do. To reduce your unique qualifications, your incomparable experience and wisdom to a spreadsheet, so all are apples—no oranges allowed—and the lowest price wins.

It's your job to resist like mad. To kick and scream and push back in every way you can. To make your branding and relationship-building so strong that that client can't wait to see your submittal, no matter what form it's written on. Write your project descriptions so that the unique value you bring stands out clear and proud. Your firm truly is unique. Don't let some standard form reduce it to a commodity.

NURTURE YOUR NETWORK

We're a greedy lot, we humans, always looking for something for ourselves. As business developers we tend to be no better.

We build a network of friends, associates and business connections in order to feed our needs. We want leads, referrals, advice, introductions, references, tips and, most importantly, a steady supply of profitable work. You rely on your network to feed you, but what have you done lately for your network?

There is a great little book that was written more than 20 years ago titled, "All I Really Need to Know I Learned in Kindergarten." Author Robert Fulghum made the premise that life is about getting along with others and playing well together in the sandbox, all of which we learned by the age of five. One of those important, early lessons was the realization that, if I want something from you, I'd better be prepared to give you what you want too. Your Mom and the kindergarten teacher called it 'sharing' and they were onto something big.

There is a natural human tendency to reciprocate behavior. If I do you a favor, you're motivated to return it. If I pop you in the nose, I can anticipate a black eye sometime soon. Without intending to sound manipulative, as business developers we can take advantage of this by planting seeds of kindness, consideration, thoughtfulness and assistance. Like the movie a few years back called, 'Pay It Forward,' we can invest in our network and build up an equity balance that will pay dividends for years to come.

The point is, your network is like an invaluable garden that produces an abundance of food—IF you tend to it regularly. But it's up to you to plant, water and fertilize it first, Only then does the garden reward your efforts.

How do you invest in your network? Start by simply **staying in touch.** If you only show up when there's some benefit to be gained, your network loses interest in you pretty quickly. If you're on your way to a meeting with Client A and you find yourself driving past the office of Client B, stop, stick your head in the door, and say 'Hi!' Don't try to sell anything, don't ask about future projects, just say a simple, 'I was thinking about you and wanted to say hello.' Trust me, you'll make their day!

Say 'Please.' When you're asking for anything, don't forget your manners. We tend to remember them at the dinner table but somehow forget that they're just as important in the business world. If you listen to most business conversations, you'll find that word conspicuous by its absence.

Say 'Thank you.' You can never say 'thank you' too many times. Express your gratitude for the friendships you enjoy, the assistance and guidance you're given, the revenue you depend on and the sustainability of your business because of the people with whom you work. Your mother was right: 'please' and 'thank you' really are magic words.

Pay attention to what's going on in the worlds of those in your network. Then, when you see an opportunity to help out with a lead, an introduction, a reference, a referral or even a job, jump on the chance to offer it. Even if it's nothing more than a pat on the back to lend moral support when someone is facing a challenge, the fact that you're paying attention will mean the world to them.

Give back. We spend so much time asking. Asking for a job, a lead, an introduction, valuable information. So when you've plucked a fresh, juicy tomato from your network 'garden,' make sure you return the favor. You may not always be able to return in kind, but there will always be a way for you to pay it back. I know a business developer who once arranged for some leftover lumber to be delivered to a client's son's Scout Troop so they could build a kitchen shelter for their campsite. A simple gesture, but much appreciated.

Your network of close friends and business associates is your lifeline. It feeds you work, it connects you to opportunity and it supports you when you are hurting. But a network doesn't come looking for you. You have to seek it out, develop it, pay attention to it, feed it and nurture it. Have you watered your garden lately?

IS YOUR SCOPE WELL-DEFINED?

Although I kick and scream in protest, it's a fact that your proposal often ends up forming an integral part of your contract with the client. Assuming that neither you nor your client like unpleasant surprises, it serves you well to ensure that the scope of services you're proposing is well-defined.

One of the best ways of delineating your services is through a *Work Breakdown Structure*. A WBS allows you to organize a large complex undertaking into a collection of bite-sized pieces that can be understood, priced, assigned and tracked.

While a WBS is an invaluable tool when you're managing the project, it's equally useful in marketing and business development. Not only can it communicate scope to a client, it clearly identifies all the tasks that are necessary to get the project done. If your client is whining about costs, you can easily point out what happens when you cut scope.

The Scope of Services in your proposal should essentially be a set of five lists.

1. What are the services to be included?
    This is done best with a detailed listing or a Work Breakdown Structure.

2. What are the services that are specifically excluded?
    Those items that are not included should be spelled out in detail. For example:
    The study will make use of available data, visual observations and interviews with end users. It will not include extensive research into the detailed system parameters, load calculations or drawing updates.

3. What are the services that are optionally available?
    Services or approaches that are outside the scope of work need to be
    identified and offered to the client as choices.
    For example:

    > *At your discretion, the City may choose for us to pursue an
    > alternate design approach, which our visual inspection of the
    > project site has identified.*
    > *We feel this alternate design approach can provide significant
    > savings in long term operating costs but could increase initial
    > construction costs by as much as five percent.*

4. What are the services that will be provided at no charge?
    Everybody likes 'free' stuff. So why not provide your client with
    'free' services? Before you get up in arms about the ethics of
    providing free professional services, let's make sure we understand
    the definition of 'free.' 'Free' means the charge is not a line item on
    your bill. The mints on the pillow at the Ritz Carlton are 'free.' The
    first three years of scheduled maintenance on your new car are also
    'free.' What might you include as 'free' when providing your
    services?
    How about:
    The following services will be provided at no charge:
    *   *The first five client-initiated change orders*
    *   *Rendered 3D model for use by your Marketing Department*
    *   *Representation at two public meetings*
    *   *Post completion inspection at six months after start-up*
    By offering these small items at 'no charge,' you increase the
    perceived value of the overall service you provide.

5. The set of deliverables the client can expect upon completion. This
    should be in the form of a detailed list to protect you from
    assumptions.
    For example:

    > *The deliverables from this project will be:*
    > 1. *Written project plan presented at the kickoff meeting.*
    > 2. *Development and maintenance of a project schedule.*
    > 3. *A written description of the construction guidelines compatible
    >   with the technology to be installed.*
    > 4. *Drawings of cable and terminal installations.*
    > 5. *Requirements for installation of cable and terminals.*
    > 6. *Detailed cable and terminal specifications.*
    > 7. *RFP and addenda for supply of cable and terminals.*

8. *Written requirements for documentation of cable and terminal installation including cable records, testing and as-built drawings.*

There isn't one of us who doesn't have scars on the tush from being bitten by assumptions. A well-defined scope in your proposal is a first line of defense against future bites.

WHAT DO YOU SELL?

Despite appearances, Rolex doesn't sell watches. Sure, that $25,000 thing on your wrist is capable of letting you know that it's a quarter past two. But so will the Timex that you bought at Sears for $19.95. No, Rolex doesn't sell watches. They sell prestige.

While we're at it, Starbucks doesn't sell coffee; they sell a second home and a lifestyle. The University of Phoenix doesn't sell university degrees. They sell a second chance.

All of which raises the question: What do you sell? Certainly not engineering or architecture. And if you don't actually sell what you've always thought you did, how can you determine what you do, in fact sell?

Let's start by looking at the world from behind the desk of one of your clients: You're the mayor of a municipality that is experiencing issues with its waste treatment plant. You've been placed under a consent decree by the EPA, you're taking calls at dinner time from Mrs. McNaughton who is wondering why sewage is backing up in her basement and you're fighting an uphill battle against a tough opponent in a re-election campaign. You don't want an engineer. You want someone who will remove your stress and let you get back to kissing babies.

What if you're the Facility Manager for a pharmaceutical plant installing a new production line? You don't want an engineer, you want the peace of mind that comes from knowing that everything is going to go smoothly and you won't lose your job because you've picked the wrong provider. You not only want all personal risk removed, you want to come out looking like a hero.

There's an important message in the fact that no one ever excitedly saves up to hire the engineer or the architect. They want the end results—the clean water, the safe streets, the reduced energy costs and the commodious spaces.

But the means to that end—the architect or engineer – is simply a necessary evil.

Let your client know that you see past the engineering scope to what we've called the 'need behind the need.' Here's an excerpt from an actual RFP:

The City intends to commission the services of a qualified A/E firm to develop concept plans for the overall design of a new aquatic center and recreation facility to be placed before the public at a referendum in November.

A predictable Statement of Understanding might state:

Smith and Jones understands that the City requires a qualified A/E firm to develop concept plans for the overall design of a new aquatic center and recreation facility. In addition, these plans will be used to present to the public in a referendum in November.

Predictable and banal. Instead, show the client that you <u>truly</u> understand the challenge they face, that you see the need behind the need, and that your services will provide a solution to their real problem. In that case you might write:

At Smith and Jones we've spent considerable time investigating the details and circumstances surrounding the new aquatic center and recreation facility. With the level of public support for this project currently at about 50/50 we know that the City will not only need an attractive and functional design, you will require a compelling and enthusiastic presentation at the public meeting prior to the referendum in November. We intend to work not only with your staff, but with your Council members as well in order to make the design work together with public opinion so this project can be a success.

A statement like this demonstrates that you have insight behind the mere checklist of things to be done. You're willing to become an active team member who not only provides design and technical expertise, but also contributes to the solution of the 'big picture.'

The Rolex buyer doesn't really care about how well the gears and springs inside work. They take that part for granted. But they care mightily about the prestige that comes from wearing one.

ANTI-COMMODITY BRANDING

Heard it again last week: "Our clients are increasingly treating us like we're a commodity!"

Yes they are. And why shouldn't they?

The economic definition of a commodity is any product or service for which, in the perception of the buyer, the only difference between one supplier or another is price. One bushel of wheat is exactly the same as another whether it was grown on the Russian steppes or the Canadian prairies. And one Civil Engineer or Architect or Contractor is the same as another. Right?

I can feel you bristling from here!

But let's be frank, if your firm is like most, the only time a prospective client encounters you is when you respond to their RFP. Your proposal is one of many in a big stack, all competing in "the Battle of the Lists," where your list of projects is pitted against the others. Be honest, if you were a client, wouldn't you select on price too?

There is good news though. It lies in that definition when we said, "in the perception of the buyer..." While it's pretty hard to make one bushel of wheat any different from another, it's very easy to make your firm stand out from the rest as something very special indeed. But the onus is on you to communicate those differences.

The biggest opportunity you have to fight the trend towards commoditization is to proactively and aggressively build your firm's brand. It's the easiest, least expensive and most powerful marketing tool you've got. But it's also the least understood and least utilized among design and construction professionals.

What is your brand? It's the sum of all the perceptions and experiences that reside within the hearts and minds of clients, prospects and indeed your entire market. In other words, it's not what you are; it's what the people who do and who might hire you think you are.

While the clients you actually work with have a front row seat as they develop those perceptions and experiences, the rest of the market—those people you hope will hire you in the future—can only judge you based on what they encounter in their world.

Imagine the view from behind the eyeballs of a prospective client who may or may not have heard of your firm. Their exposure to you consists of a Qualifications package filled with boilerplate, a call from a business developer who has obviously got word that you might have a project on the street and is anxious to build an instant relationship, and a proposal in response to your RFP. When a long parade of firms suddenly shows up at your door, all claiming to be uniquely qualified but all looking and sounding the same, you don't have much on which to build a really informed perception.

Brand building takes place over long periods of time. Think about the big names—Apple, Disney, American Express. They've all invested millions of dollars over many years to teach you about their companies and their products. Those branding messages have been both carefully crafted and relentless. Which makes it very easy to sell you their products and services when it comes your time to buy.

But if you'd never heard of them before, they'd have a hard time convincing you that you should stand in a long line or fill out an application form before they charged you a premium for what they sell.

You can influence the perception of your buyers to where your firm is seen as something different from all the rest. A well-orchestrated branding effort that uses advertising, direct mail, public relations, social media and other select tools is an anti-commodity investment that will return many times its cost.

TYPOS, TRUTH AND TRUST

That last chapter formed the message of a blog I sent out a while back. But when the blog went out, the headline didn't say, "Anti-commodity branding," instead it introduced a whole new word and announced, "Anit-commodity branding."

That's a rather blatant spelling mistake! And in the headline of all places! So go ahead, point and laugh at the marketing guy who can't spell check his own work. I'm fair game.

Don't you just love it when you stick your foot in it? In front of a huge audience no less? There's no doubt that messing up is a fact of life. I do it. You do it. We all do it from time to time.

It's particularly embarrassing to mess up when you're doing paid work for a client. But having egg all over your face offers one of life's prime moments to set yourself apart and make some truly large marketing strides with your client.

When you've dropped the ball you have two choices. The first is to hide, play dumb and deny all knowledge and responsibility. This tends to work for a moment but then things go downhill fast as it becomes rapidly apparent that you are the guilty party.

Your second choice is to own up to your blunder even before your client has noticed. When this second approach is paired with a, "And here's what I'm going to do to fix it..." you gain huge helpings of credibility and build even more resilience into that relationship.

Trust is the foundation of all great relationships. When you volunteer information that has the potential to make you look bad, the client can only think, "If she is honest with me about this, it's pretty easy to assume she's honest with me about everything." And the trust grows.

Trust is not a commodity. It's a precious gift that is earned slowly, over a long period of time. Clients the world over are willing to pay a premium for it. They're willing to go out of their way to work with a firm and with professionals who have earned their trust. So next time you drop the ball, stick your foot in it, or otherwise screw up, 'fess up. You'll be amazed at the reaction.

LET'S AGREE ON AT LEAST THIS MUCH

It's so easy to get sidelined in any discussion about winning work when people get wrapped around the axle of definitions. We waste so much valuable time splitting hairs over the difference between marketing and sales that we skillfully manage to avoid doing either. So this week we're going to clear it all up once and for all.

While you might have some subtly different definitions, let's at least agree on these meanings for purposes of the discussions we have in this book.

Marketing

This is the big, umbrella term that includes any and every activity you might undertake that is going to help bring in work. If you're taking a prospective client to lunch, that's part of marketing. If it's 2 AM and you're working to get a last minute proposal out, that's part of marketing. If you're staffing a booth or making a presentation at a trade show, that's part of marketing. Under that broad umbrella, there are a number of more specialized activities.

Brand Building

This is the phase in which you educate your entire target market about who you are, what you sell, who you sell it to and—most importantly—what sets you apart from all the others who want to sell the same thing into the same market. Branding is not intended to win projects. It's supposed to build name recognition, enhance your reputation and build mind share across your market.

Business Development

This is the proactive development of one-to-one relationships between two people who want to do business together. We know that this is a relationship-based business. Nobody is going to sign on for your $100K fee without first having the opportunity to get to know you, find out what makes you tick, watch you in action and see your ethics at work. And we're not talking about getting to know your firm in a generic way. Business development is face-to-face: across the table at a restaurant, serving together on the same committee and watching you blow that short putt on the 8th green.

Sales

This is where we get down to the nitty-gritty to convince a client to hire you instead of them for this particular project at this particular time. Selling is expensive. It involves costly and time-consuming proposals, interviews, sales calls and pricing, all focused specifically on one particular project. Because it's so expensive to sell a project you want to be selective about those you choose to chase.

How do these various pieces of the marketing puzzle fit together? Brand building aims far out into the future—at least two or three years. It educates your market, keeps you in the front of their minds and helps them become positively predisposed to considering your firm when it's project time. Business development aims at the middle ground—six months or so into the future. It lets the client get to know you as a person and build a preference for you when selection time comes around.

Sales focuses on the short term—30 to 60 days—and creates a compelling argument as to why you should be selected for this particular project. It removes potential objections, shows how your firm brings more value than the rest and closes the deal.

The dirty little secret about marketing is that it's dead simple. Nothing complicated about it at all. Just a few simple pieces that, when assembled in sequence and used consistently and appropriately, work endless miracles.

A SNEAK PEEK AT THE NEXT BOOK—

HOW FAST DO YOU FAIL?

A 12-month-old baby knows a lot about failure. Every time she lets go of the coffee table to attempt a step or two – thump! Failed again. Of course the easiest way for our cute little one to avoid failure is to give up on the idea of walking. It would be so much easier to just sit and let someone bring the bottle.

There are a couple of reasons why that toddler keeps trying. First, the world looks pretty big and exciting and you can cover a lot more ground on two feet than on all fours, so it's worth the effort. But more importantly, she hasn't yet got the memo that failure is a bad thing. There's no shame in falling on your butt when you're 12 months old. In fact we grown-ups think it's pretty darn cute.

But by the time we've grown up, been formally educated, got a job and taken responsibility for an engineering firm, they've managed to thoroughly convince us that failure is the worst possible option, to be avoided at all costs. And that's when most growth and learning stops.

Most design firms that I see spend an inordinate effort to avoid failure of any kind. Which, don't get me wrong, is a pretty good idea when you're designing a bridge or a building. But it's a major obstacle when you're trying to grow a company. By assiduously avoiding failure, we also avoid innovation, creativity, growth and breakthrough thinking. We stay carefully in the rut we occupy and discourage looking from side to side.

The best companies on the other hand, the ones we all wish we could be like, encourage, embrace and endure failure on their way to success. And the faster they fail, the quicker they grow. The February, 2014 issue of Fast Company (if you aren't a regular reader, you should be) includes an article about a startup cosmetics company that maintains

113

a core group of customers, known as the Idea Lab, to whom they turn for feedback on new ideas. According to founder Jane Park, a former Starbucks executive, "Lab feedback can be brutally honest; only about a third of [our ideas] make it to market. The idea of failing fast has been part of our DNA."

Painfully few firms seek regular feedback from their clients. Even fewer invite their clients and end users into the decision making process as they evolve their companies. Of the thousands of firms I've encountered I would estimate that fewer than 10 percent even have an outside member on their Board of Directors.

It's only with regular, brutally honest feedback that you can evolve your firm to keep pace with the needs of your clients. By inviting your clients to join you behind the curtain where the strategic decisions are made you'll feel freer to experiment, try, fail, try again and get it right.

Wanna fail faster?

- Set up a Board of Advisors entirely made up of people from outside your firm.
- Establish a Brain Trust, whose job it is to push you into places you might not be brave enough to go on your own.
- Host quarterly client feedback forums in which they feel free to tell you what they really think and share the great ideas that are apparent from the other side of the table.
- Invite active input and swift, timely response from your clients, and then rapidly incorporate that feedback into the ongoing evolution of your services.
- Fail regularly, then get up, brush yourselves off and carry on, having learned invaluable lessons.

That toddler knows far more about failure than you or I do and she's not afraid of it. That's why she learns faster, grows quicker and laughs more often. When was the last time you were glad you fell on your ass?

ABOUT DAVID STONE

One of the leading marketing thinkers in the AEC industry, David Stone has advised hundreds of design and construction firms around the globe ranging in size from one person to $2 billion in annual revenue. He is the author of 15 books and is a sought-after speaker at design and construction conferences around the world.

With a career that began in architecture in the mid-70s, David has held every position from Draftsman to Principal. He has witnessed and dealt with the massive changes this industry faces and continues to explore new ways to promote and sell design and construction services.

He and his wife Gail divide their time between Savannah, GA and Vancouver, BC.

Welcome to blüStone Marketing, Inc.

bluStone Marketing, Inc. (formerly Stone and Company) provides consulting, training and coaching in marketing, business development and sales for professionals in the architecture and engineering professions.

We work with private design firms and the many associations representing them. Our largest client has annual revenues in excess of $2 billion. Our smallest has been a one-person operation. We have worked in 49 our of 50 states (please help us make it all 50!), 7 our of 10 Canadian provinces and half the populated continents.

Made in the USA
Monee, IL
07 July 2026

56552303R00066